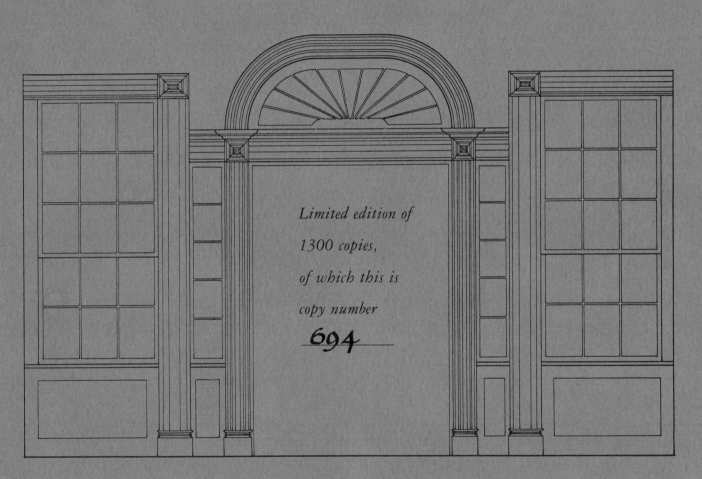

Limited edition of
1300 copies,
of which this is
copy number
694

D. Gregory Jeane

Douglas Clare Purcell

The Architectural Legacy
of the Lower Chattahoochee Valley
in Alabama and Georgia

The Architectural Legacy of the Lower Chattahoochee Valley in Alabama and Georgia

D. Gregory Jeane
EDITOR

Douglas Clare Purcell
ASSOCIATE EDITOR

Sidney R. Mullen, *Principal Architect*

George R. McGlaun, Jr., *Photographer*

A Bicentennial Project published for the

Historic Chattahoochee Commission by

The University of Alabama Press, University, Alabama

Published in honor of the
American Revolution Bicentennial, 1776–1976
under the auspices of the

Alabama Bicentennial Commission

and
under the endorsement of the

Georgia Bicentennial Commission

for

The Historic Chattahoochee Commission

Library of Congress Cataloging in Publication Data
Main entry under title:

The Architectural legacy of the Lower Chattahoochee
    Valley in Alabama and Georgia.

    Bibliography: p.
    Includes index.
    1. Architecture—Alabama—Chattahoochee.
2. Architecture—Georgia—Chattahoochee. 3. Architecture—Details. I. Jeane, D. Gregory. II. Purcell, Douglas Clare. III. Historic Chattahoochee
Commission.
NA730.A22C463   720'.9758.   77-27594
ISBN 0-8173-6002-6

CONTENTS

3/24/80 · mwu

HISTORIC CHATTAHOOCHEE COMMISSION

Board of Directors
Mr. Robert Bennett, Sr.
Mrs. Claude Milford
Mrs. Alice Doughtie
Mr. William W. Nordan
Mr. Fred Watson
Dr. Allen M. Pearson
Mr. Charles Tigner
Mr. Sam Singer
Mrs. Jenny Copeland
Mr. Marvin Singletary
Mrs. Florence Foy Strang
Mrs. Ruth Crump
Mr. Creel Richardson
Mr. Steve Elliott
Mr. Larry Register
Mrs. Jan Dempsey
Mr. Reginald Cain
Mrs. Janice Biggers
Mr. Gary Ford

Georgia Advisory Members
Lt. Colonel (Ret.) Dick Grube
Mrs. India Wilson
Mrs. Yates Cathrall
Mrs. Victoria Custer
Mrs. Elizabeth Stapleton
Mrs. Marion Roberts

HCC Officers
Mr. Larry Register, Chairman
Dr. Allen M. Pearson, Vice-Chairman
Mrs. Jean Robinson, Secretary
Mr. James S. Clark, Treasurer
Mr. Douglas C. Purcell, Executive Director

Past Board of Directors
Mrs. Hortense Balkcom
Dr. H. Floyd Vallery
Mrs. Ann Smith
Mr. Harold Coulter
Mrs. Dorothy Powell
Mr. W. V. Neville, Jr.
Mr. Edward W. Neal
Mrs. J. Walter Jones

Past Georgia Advisory Member
Mrs. W. Norton Roberts

ACKNOWLEDGMENTS

This book results from the work of many interested, dedicated individuals and organizations. The Historic Chattahoochee Commission initiated and constantly sustained the project. Auburn University has proved supportive; The University of Alabama Press has encouraged publication. The endorsement of the project by the Bicentennial Commission of Alabama and the Georgia Commission for the National Bicentennial Celebration has been appreciated.

The idea for the work was developed by Dr. H. Floyd Vallery, Assistant to the President, Auburn University. Dr. Vallery served as Project Chairman during his tenure on the HCC Board of Directors and contributed his valuable insight from his early association with the project, his continued suggestions, and his enthusiasm. Douglas C. Purcell, Executive Director of the Historic Chattahoochee Commission and associate editor of the book, constantly provided invaluable assistance. His ceaseless efforts in obtaining information on the structures, his tactful pressure to meet deadlines, and his never failing understanding when they couldn't be met deserve special thanks. Without his constant revision of the fate of the structures, this book would be less accurate. Ed Bagwell, Acting Chairman of the Department of Geography, Auburn University, has graciously not overloaded my schedule to permit writing of the manuscript. The Commission's Board of Directors has shown patience and understanding of the delays; Mrs. Florence Foy Strang has been especially kind and encouraging.

Unless otherwise noted all photographs are the work of George R. McGlaun, Jr., whose keen eye for detail is evident.

With the exception of four drawings, all architectural renderings were done by Sidney R. Mullen, AIA, who has a particular skill for working with historical detail. Ed Neal, a prominent Columbus architect and his associates rendered the drawings of the Woolfolk and Tingle houses. The Bullard-Hart House drawings were done by Hecht and Burdeshaw Architects of Columbus. The Hoxey (Lion) House drawings were made by Pound, Flowers and Dedwylder Architects of Columbus. A special thanks is due the West Georgia Chapter of the AIA for their enthusiasm and support for the project.

So many individuals assisted in this project that it is impossible to list them here. Breaking with tradition, I have included a special appendix in the back of the book that identifies every person who helped gather information on each of the structures. In this small way I thank them all for their commitment and effort.

With gratitude I thank my former professors Milton B. Newton, Jr., and Fred B. Kniffen for awakening in me an appreciation for all the material things human beings have placed upon the landscape, which give it character.

A word of thanks is appropriate to my typist, Miss Terry Oswalt, who has patiently typed, proofed, and retyped my seemingly incessant changes. She has been an invaluable help.

Lastly, without the love and support of my wife Karen this book would have been yet unfinished. She remained patient with my hours away in the field, library, and office. There is no substitute for long evenings alone; I am grateful.

PREFACE

Architectural restoration and preservation are currently experiencing popularity nationwide. From the small village to the megalopolis there is a beehive of restoration activity. The major drive seems to aim toward preserving those structures associated with citizens or events of greater than local magnitude. Consequently, numerous structures of architectural significance are by-passed; houses and buildings much more indicative of a general lifestyle are allowed to decay, their beauty and utility lost to future generations.

It is encouraging to note that an important recent trend in preservation is to develop villages or at least significant complexes of structures so that a past lifestyle is more readily envisioned. Williamsburg is the prototype for creating the total effect. Other similar projects include Henry Ford's village of Deerfield and Old Sturbridge Village in Massachusetts. Locally Westville, near Lumpkin, Georgia, and the Georgia Agrarama at Tifton are noteworthy.

Despite the efforts being put forth, hundreds of endangered structures waste away yearly and are threatened by imminent destruction from decay, vandalism, or progress. This volume has been assembled to preserve the history and architectural flavor of sixty-odd buildings in the Lower Chattahoochee Valley (see map on p. xv). All of the structures are examples that convey an image of life in lower Alabama and Georgia from their earliest settlement until the turn of the twentieth century. These buildings are typical, not necessarily the finest architectural gems. Each is endangered and worthy of note because of its history or style. Through narrative, photographs, and architectural drawings, this book preserves architecture that is rapidly disappearing, thus leaving a record of past styles and some indication of past lifeways.

That the effort put forth in this volume has been justified and the objective upheld can be witnessed by the record now available on buildings destroyed since the project began two years ago. Indirectly, there has been an impact on local groups to save some buildings before they were demolished. The Malone Stone House (Bainbridge, Georgia) has been razed. The Tingle Home (Columbus, Georgia) has been razed to build a service station. The Hood Law Office (Cuthbert, Georgia) was destroyed while being moved to a new site. The William Walker-Cook-Hood House has been destroyed by fire. Each of these structures has been preserved in this volume. The Kennedy Home (Abbeville, Alabama) has been saved by a local action group. The old Russell County Courthouse (Seale, Alabama) is being restored. The Trammell Home (Chambers County, Alabama) has been restored. These structures have been saved, partially through interest generated by this project.

The Historic Chattahoochee Commission, sponsor of the project, contacted each county within its jurisdiction requesting that endangered structures be submitted for consideration by the Board of Directors. Each house, church, mill, or other structure had to have local significance and be in danger of destruction. Once a building was selected for inclusion, collection of data began. Historical societies, historians, and knowledgeable people were contacted. Journals, account books, deeds, and personal correspondence provided additional information. A detailed photographic record, interior and exterior, was taken for each structure. Last, but not least, architects measured and drew scale drawings of floor plans, trim, and elevations for each building. Insofar as possible, all drawings are an effort to re-create the original plans and elevations; additions are evident from the photographs.

A useful and permanent record of the architectural heritage has been compiled for the following counties in the Lower Chattahoochee Valley: Georgia—Chattahoochee, Clay, Decatur, Early, Harris, Muscogee, Quitman, Randolph, Seminole, Stewart, and Troup; Alabama—Barbour, Chambers, Dale, Henry, Houston, Lee, and Russell. It is hoped that attention will be focused on buildings that may yet be saved. For those structures included in the project and beyond redemption, the book stands as a valuable source of data concerning appearance, size, construction details, and ownership. In addition, something of the way their inhabitants used them leads one to a better understanding of past lifestyles. Precise architectural and historical information on representative structures should be of value for future planning, not only of buildings but also of communities.

D. GREGORY JEANE
Opelika, Alabama

Dedicated to all persons who hold that restoration, preservation, and creation of beauty form a worthy endeavor; that to preserve part of our cultural heritage through the medium of architecture is a noble concern.

Numbers refer to site of structure.

ALABAMA

Barbour County
1. Vicksburg and Brunswick Depot
2. Alexander Home and Outbuildings
3. Barbour County High School
4. Octagon House
5. Jennings Home

Chambers County
6. Barrow Home
7. Trammell Home

Dale County
8. Dowling-Holman Home

Henry County
9. Kennedy Home
10. Liberty Methodist Church Grave Shelter
11. Pelham House
12. Mills House
13. Gray House
14. Saddlebag House
15. Graham House

Houston County
16. Columbia Jailhouse

Lee County
17. Meadows Mill
18. Edwards Home
19. Antioch Methodist Church Grave Shelter
20. Neva Winston Home
21. Gold Hill Commissary
22. Wagnon-Mitchell-Samford Store
23. Houston-Dunn House
24. A. D. McLain Building

Russell County
25. Mitchell-Ferrell Home
26. Russell County Courthouse
27. Mount Lebanon Baptist Church Grave Shelter
28. Hyram Cemetery Grave Shelters
29. Christian Log House
30. Goodhope Baptist Church
31. Uchee Methodist Church
32. Crawford Grave Shelter
33. Bank of Seale

GEORGIA

Chattahoochee County
34. Liberty Hill Methodist Church

Clay County
35. Dill House

Decatur County
36. Coleman-Vickers Home
37. Malone Stone House

Early County
38. Coheelee Creek Bridge

Harris County
39. Cleaveland-Godwin-Nelson-Peacock Home
40. William Walker-Cook-Hood House
41. Bethany Baptist Church Grave Shelter
42. Cleaveland-Godwin-Nelson-Peacock Barn

Muscogee County
43. Hoxey Home
44. Bullard-Hart Home
45. Tingle Home
46. Woolfolk Home

Quitman County
47. Quitman County Jail

Randolph County
48. Hood Law Office
49. Key Gazebo-Greenhouse

Seminole County
50. Sikes-George House

Stewart County
51. Wood's Home
52. Moye Plantation Outbuildings
53. Providence Chapel Grave Shelter

Troup County
54. Rutledge House
55. Frost-Gray Home

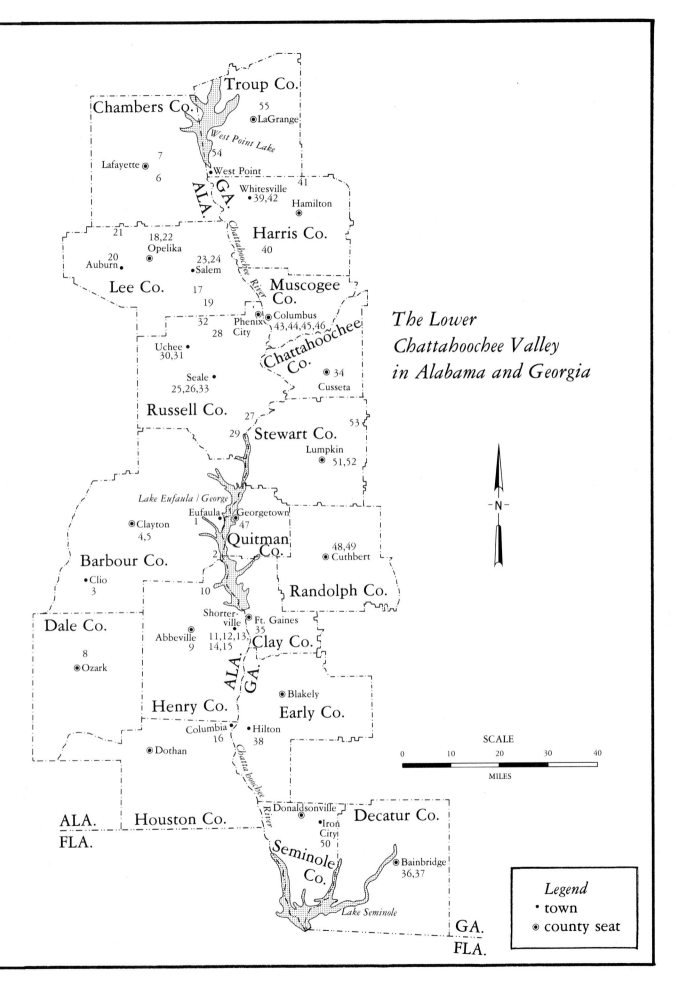

The Lower
Chattahoochee Valley
in Alabama and Georgia

Troup Co.

Chambers Co.

55
⊙LaGrange

West Point Lake

54

Lafayette ⊙ 7
        6

•West Point

41

Whitesville
•39,42   Hamilton ⊙

GA.
ALA.

Chattahoochee River

21 18,22
Opelika
20 ⊙

Auburn • 23,24
        •Salem

Harris Co.
40

Lee Co. 17
        19

32

28

Muscogee
Co.

Phenix ⊙Columbus
City   43,44,45,46

Chattahoochee Co.

Uchee •
30,31

Seale •
25,26,33

Russell Co.

⊙ 34
Cusseta

27

29

Stewart Co.

53

Lumpkin
⊙ 51,52

Lake Eufaula / George

Eufaula • ⊙Georgetown
1 •   47

⊙Clayton
4,5

2

Quitman Co.

48,49
⊙Cuthbert

Barbour Co.

• Clio
3

10

Randolph Co.

Dale Co.

Shorter-
ville •
⊙ • Ft. Gaines
Abbeville 11,12,13, 35
9   14,15 Clay Co.

8
⊙Ozark

ALA.
GA.

Henry Co.

⊙ Blakely

Early Co.

Columbia •
16   • Hilton
     38

⊙ Dothan

Chattahoochee River

SCALE

0   10   20   30   40

MILES

ALA.
FLA.

Houston Co.

Donaldsonville
⊙ • Iron
    City
    50

Decatur Co.

Seminole
Co.

⊙ Bainbridge
36,37

Lake Seminole

GA.
FLA.

Legend
• town
⊙ county seat

-N-

*The Architectural Legacy
of the Lower Chattahoochee Valley
in Alabama and Georgia*

Introduction

THIS BOOK ATTEMPTS to be inclusive with respect to various architectural structures. However, all styles are not represented because the emphasis is upon achieving a meld of structures so that churches, stores, schools, and other interesting structures are not overshadowed by undue stress on houses. All too often houses are covered to the exclusion of other important buildings. In addition to numerous houses is a variety of commercial buildings including: a depot, bank, general store, commissary, and gristmill. Attention has also been devoted to churches and to grave shelters, jails, and a covered bridge.

For decades house types have been the core of research for a number of professions. The study of houses may seem a bit strange as a form of scientific endeavor, but dwellings are an element of culture that can be effectively used in analyzing regional differences. Housing is a basic need of human beings, and the type of house built reflects cultural heritage, current fashion, and functional needs, as well as other attributes of man's cultural milieu. The quest for origins of types continues; definitive works are rare. I have made an attempt to synthesize a number of approaches into a meaningful dialogue, and every effort has been made to ensure that generalizations are based on fact, not supposition. Bibliographic notes have been kept to a minimum and are at the end of each chapter; a selected bibliography is also included.

The text is divided into six chapters: folk houses, early central-hall houses, Greek Revival architecture, Victorian architecture, and architectural potpourri I and II. Each chapter has a brief introduction that defines the style in question. Any differences of opinion are also

noted in order that the reader will not accidentally be led to conclude that architectural history is cut and dry. The last two chapters are designated as potpourri because they include a variety of structures that are singly representative of a style or that lack any specific characteristics by which to pigeonhole them in standard historical periods. Under no circumstances are they relegated to the last for lack of architectural merit or historical significance. Where possible all pertinent data submitted by interested parties have been used. To avoid repetition architectural narratives do not necessarily incorporate the same items in any given order. Instead, those features that are unique or that give special character have been emphasized.

CHAPTER ONE

Folk Houses

THE EARLIEST PRIMITIVE pioneer cabins are now extremely rare in the Lower Chattahoochee Valley. These dwellings have been superseded by permanent, substantial, and traditional first-generation log houses, of which many examples still exist. Succeeding first-generation log houses were more relaxed in style and in turn were replaced by houses of frame construction. With the use of lumber and balloon framing as a more refined and modern style, there followed a decline of the more complex techniques in log construction. A period of change continued as newer methods of building and materials replaced the old. The stages of this evolution can be designated as pioneer, first generation, second generation, and third generation.[1] The traditional Abraham Lincoln birthplace at Hodgenville, Kentucky, is an example of the pioneer cabin, and probably its Alabama and Georgia contemporaries would have been quite similar. Built according to a definite plan and style, it had dimensions of approximately 18 x 16 feet, a size that was common in the Southeast. The first-generation houses that followed exhibited fine workmanship, great strength, and durability. Clearly, a difference was evident between the cabin and the log house: the cabin was an expedient, temporary shelter; the log house was built with care and skill to endure, and many have, for more than 150 years.

The basic house types were determined by their plan and include the *single pen,* the *double pen,* the *dogtrot,* and the *saddlebag.* Typologically, the single-pen log house was derived from the old English one-bay house and was the oldest type of folk house in the Deep South. Rectangular in floor plan, it was one story with a small loft and had a gable roof, an exterior chimney centered at the gable side, a front entrance centered in a longer wall, and a rear door usually directly opposite; in the Chattahoochee Valley windows commonly were on either side of the chimney. Placing two log single pens together formed the double house. If the second pen abutted the clear gable side wall, the double pen resulted. If the second pen was placed at the gable side but was separated from the first by a space of 10 to 12 feet, which was then roofed over, the house type was the dogtrot house, with a central passage, or "dogtrot." To form the saddlebag type, the second pen was positioned against the chimney end.

Single Pen

The first-generation single-pen log house (ca. 1810–1840), usually rectangular and rather large (20 to 25 feet on the front and rear, 16 to 19 feet on the side), had large, carefully hewn, plank-shaped wall logs with the half-dovetail, and sometimes with the V and square corners. It had a relatively spacious loft (the loft joints were mortised into the front and rear walls) and a chimney of rock or ashlar rather than brick. The piers were not of brick; rock or blocks of wood served this purpose even in later generations.

Second-generation single-pen houses (ca. 1840–1940) had additional space provided by frame appendages of milled lumber. The log portion was usually smaller than in first-generation houses, and brick piers and brick chimneys were sometimes used. North Alabama house builders continued using hewn logs, although they usually left the bark intact on the top and the bottom of the log. In the Coastal Plain, single-pen houses of the late nineteenth century were often built of split pine logs, half-round portion facing out and flat side facing in. An example of the second-generation single-pen house is the Gray House near Shorterville, Henry County, Alabama (Figure 1, Section B).

Third-generation single-pen houses (ca. 1870–1930) were of frame and weatherboarding, although hewn sills, possibly from earlier log houses, were used occasionally. Often, a third outside door was present in the gable side opposite the fireplace. The house normally had piers and chimneys of brick; sash windows and hardware were standard. In addition to the rear shed room, the house often had a small room on one side of the front porch. Metal roofing was common on the frame single-pen houses, but shingles probably continued in use for many years.

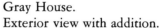

Gray House.
Exterior view with addition.

Gray House.
Detail of siding and corner notching.

Gray House.
Original structure with addition removed.

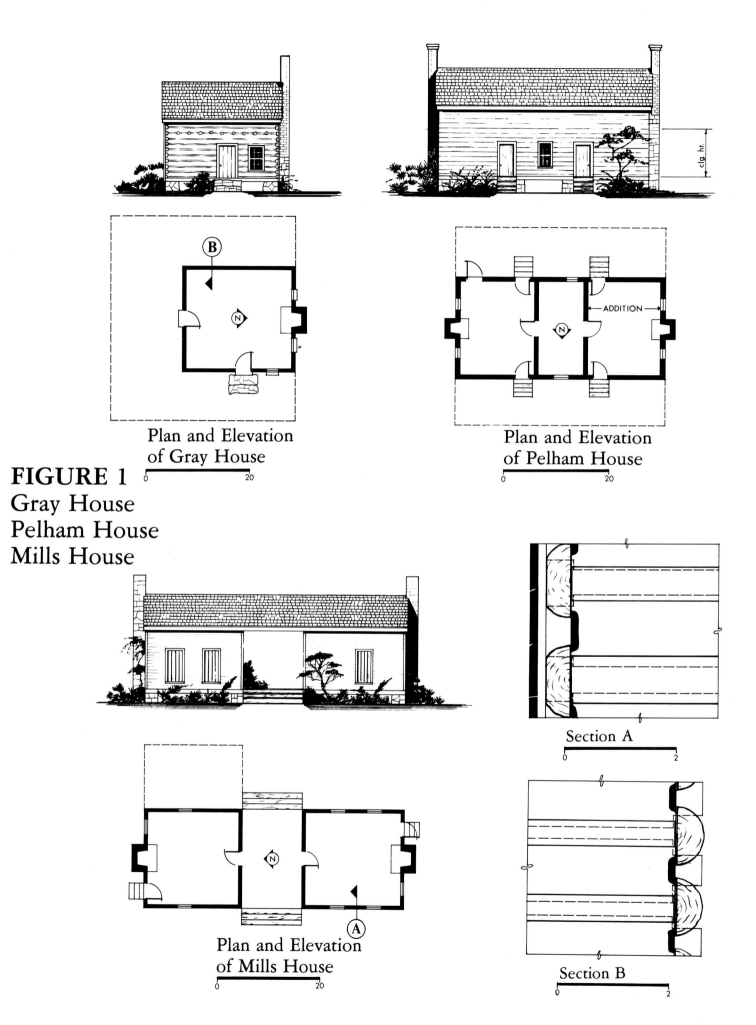

Plan and Elevation
of Gray House

Plan and Elevation
of Pelham House

FIGURE 1
Gray House
Pelham House
Mills House

Section A

Plan and Elevation
of Mills House

Section B

Dogtrot House

First-generation dogtrot houses (ca. 1810–1840) had large rectangular rooms about 19 x 17 feet, separate front doors to the log rooms in addition to the central passage, and a loft above one or both log rooms. The great width of the house front averaged about 48 feet, with some examples over 50 feet. Half-dovetail corners were most common.

Second-generation dogtrot houses (ca. 1840–1940) were defined by two square, or nearly square, log pens, usually between 16 and 19 feet for all sides. The loft area was less often used, and a separate front door in addition to the central hall was fairly common. The V corner was more frequent than was the half-dovetail corner. In place of large plank-shaped wall logs, characteristic of the first generation, logs of smaller diameter were ordinarily used. Often, second-generation houses were weatherboarded, and some examples had logs that served only as a framework for attaching exterior siding. Examples of the second-generation dogtrot type are the Mills House near Shorterville (Figure 1, Section A) and possibly the Christian Log House (Figure 2).

Third-generation dogtrot houses (ca. 1870–1930) are still, in many variations, important rural and urban dwellings in the Lower Chattahoochee Valley. Basically a reproduction of the second generation in frame and weatherboarding, the house had two main rooms that were nearly always square, averaging about 17 feet on a side. Typically, frame dogtrot houses had only one front entrance, in the passage; the house was not so long as earlier forms because pens were smaller. Open passages were common in rural areas; however, a closed passage with the front door flanked by glass panes was characteristic of the type in towns. Appendages were common, usually at the front and rear. A long addition onto one side that produced a T-plan was a variation of wide distribution. Sometimes the builders added dormer windows and front gables. Large windows replaced the separate front doors of earlier pens.

Other Folk Houses

Types of folk dwellings other than the single pen and dogtrot were not numerous enough in their early stages to establish clearly the distinct stages of development. Log double-pen and saddlebag houses were, evidently, never common, judging by the few survivors. Their frame counterparts were more abundant, particularly as urban rental houses.

DOUBLE-PEN HOUSES. A relatively small number of examples indicates that log single-pen houses were often enlarged by a frame addition at the side, one early example being the Pelham House near Shorterville, Henry County, Alabama (Figure 1). When details of individual house histories are unknown, it is not always possible to determine if the appendages were built in the nineteenth century, or later. The double pen would appear to be the simplest means of enlarging a log house and is an old solution for acquiring more space. The English one-bay house of the Tidewater underwent a similar enlargement.

SADDLEBAG HOUSES. This type was distinctive, being the only folk house with a central chimney in the Chattahoochee area; however, log examples are rare (Figure 3). The frame or third-generation form was similar to the frame dogtrot in having rooms that averaged very close to 16 x 16 feet, although these were not always square or equal in size. Front windows and separate front doors were usual except in one variety. The exception had a central front entrance into an alcove from which doors led into each front room. This arrangement was a "blind hall" entrance because the chimney blocked the passage. Like the single pen, the dogtrot, and the double pen, the saddlebag plan was represented in houses of the Maryland-Virginia Tidewater.

NONTRADITIONAL HOUSES. Three dwellings, introduced in the nineteenth and early twentieth centuries, are important because they were very popular and replaced the traditional single and double houses. These were the pyramidal-roof house, the shotgun house, and the bungalow; only the pyramidal-roof house is included in this study.

The pyramidal-roof house, generally square in plan, was introduced into Alabama sometime during the middle part of the nineteenth century as a popular house. A departure from the folk houses of the period, it nevertheless was widely adopted and by the last quarter of the nineteenth century had many variations, one of

which included an open central hallway. An example of the pyramidal-roof house type is the Graham House in Henry County, Alabama (Figure 4).

The likely prototype of the pyramidal-roof house was one of the Georgian style, represented by the Gorgas House, in Tuscaloosa, Alabama, and a number of other examples. In plan, these were symmetrical, composed basically of four equal-sized rooms, two on either side of a central hallway. Often it had two stories, although many one-story examples exist as well. Built of frame and weatherboarding or brick, the house had a hipped or pyramidal roof. The association of this type of house with higher than average economic status might explain its success as a popular dwelling. The pyramidal-roof house was also used as a two-family unit in Southern towns and for workers in lumber-mill settlements with which it has been associated.[2]

Mills House.
Exterior view.

Mills House.
Interior detail of log siding.

Mills House

No historical data are available on the past ownership of the Mills House (Figure 1). Using the criteria established by Wilson for determining folk-house types, the house can be classified as a second-generation dogtrot. The house would have been built between 1840 and 1940.

The Mills House, near Shorterville, Henry County, Alabama, is constructed on stone piers built without mortar. Sills are hand-hewn pine logs 10 inches square. Floor joists are logs notched to rest upon the sills; only the joist top has been leveled. Rafters are 3 x 4 inches. Instead of having a ridge pole, the rafters are overlapping, mitered, and joined with square pegs. The ceiling joists are small logs, flat on the bottom and notched into the wall logs. The roof is sheet metal but would originally have been wooden shingles. The exterior log walls serve as a framework for attaching weatherboarding to the side.

The interior is in poor condition. Spaces between the logs are covered with wooden strips. Flooring is of boards of random width. The ceilings are of 1 x 10 inch tongue and groove. Interestingly enough, they were painted blue, possibly from a dye made of local plants. Fireplaces and chimneys are of soft-clay bricks. Although beyond repair, the Mills House remains enough intact to indicate that it was a simple but comfortable home.

Mills House.
Fireplace detail.

Mills House.
Door detail.

Pelham House

Built ca. 1820, the Pelham House, near Shorterville, Henry County, Alabama, is representative of the oldest type of folk house in the Lower Chattahoochee Valley (Figure 1). Resting on fieldstone piers, the 8-inch sills support 8-inch log joists, and log piers under the sills provide additional support. The original single-pen log structure was enlarged by adding frame appendages and an attached front porch. The whole building is weatherboarded now. The house has a gable roof covered with tin, though shingles would have been the original roofing. The chimneys are interesting. Flared at the bottom, they are built of stone to approximately sixty percent of their height. Where the offset occurs, the remaining stack is of clay brick using common bonding. The Pelham House is a good example of an early single pen later modified to a double pen.

Pelham House.
Exterior view.

Christian Log House.
Exterior view.

Christian Log House.
Detail of notching.

Christian Log House

Although its detailed history is not extant, the Christian Log House, near Cottonton, Russell County, Alabama, is possibly an example of a second-generation dogtrot (Figure 2). The appendage off the back and the two-room-deep floor plan are definitive characteristics.

Structurally, the house is very similar to the Mills House. The sills are supported by mortared stone piers that are slightly wider at the bottom than the top. Sills are 12 x 12 inch

FIGURE 2
Christian Log House
Cottonton, Alabama

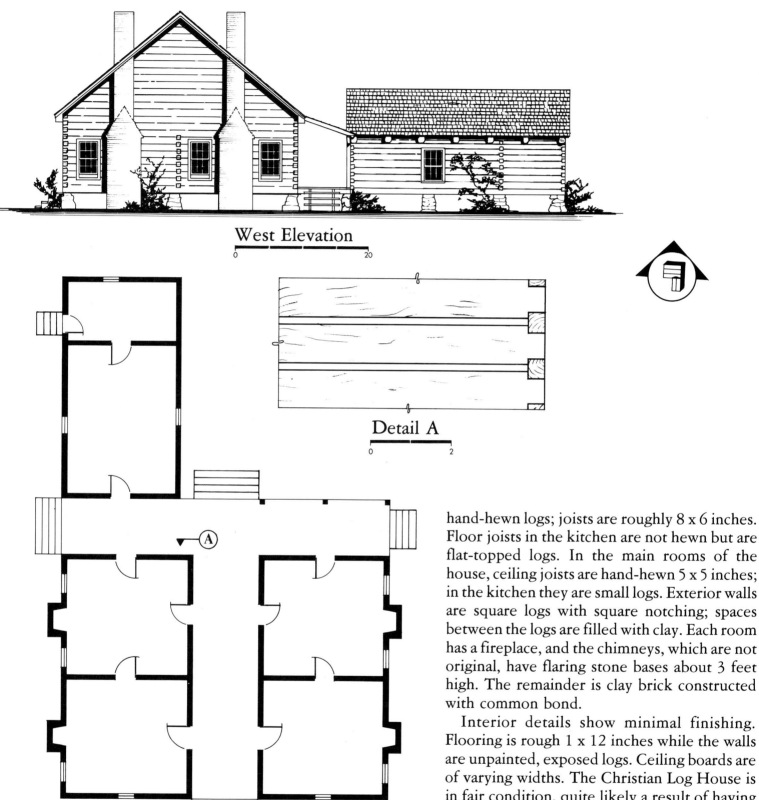

West Elevation

0   20

Detail A

0   2

Floor Plan

0   20

hand-hewn logs; joists are roughly 8 x 6 inches. Floor joists in the kitchen are not hewn but are flat-topped logs. In the main rooms of the house, ceiling joists are hand-hewn 5 x 5 inches; in the kitchen they are small logs. Exterior walls are square logs with square notching; spaces between the logs are filled with clay. Each room has a fireplace, and the chimneys, which are not original, have flaring stone bases about 3 feet high. The remainder is clay brick constructed with common bond.

Interior details show minimal finishing. Flooring is rough 1 x 12 inches while the walls are unpainted, exposed logs. Ceiling boards are of varying widths. The Christian Log House is in fair condition, quite likely a result of having been constantly inhabited. The house is plain, but typical of the average rural house in much of the South prior to the latter nineteenth century.

Christian Log House.
Detail of wall construction. Note the adze marks on the logs.

Christian Log House.
Porch and breezeway.

In Henry County, Alabama, this saddlebag house is a third-generation folk-house type as evidenced by its total frame construction (Figure 3). The house may actually have been a frame single pen with the north room added to form the saddlebag type. Such additions are difficult to date. The lumber dimensions indicate a recent construction date, i.e., 2 x 8, 2 x 4, and 2 x 6 inches. Sills and joists in older homes were substantially larger. Currently used as a storage barn for hay, the house is a typical sharecropper dwelling.

East Elevation

0   15

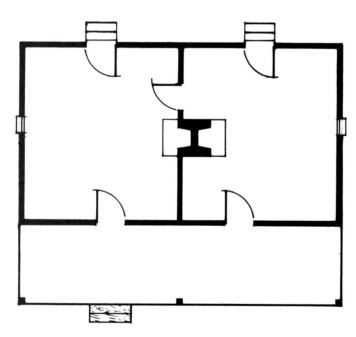

Floor Plan

0   15

FIGURE 3
A Saddlebag House
Henry County, Alabama

A saddlebag house
near Shorterville, Alabama.
Exterior view.

Graham House.
Front view.

FIGURE 4
Graham House (Pyramidal Roof)
Henry County, Alabama

West Elevation

0   20

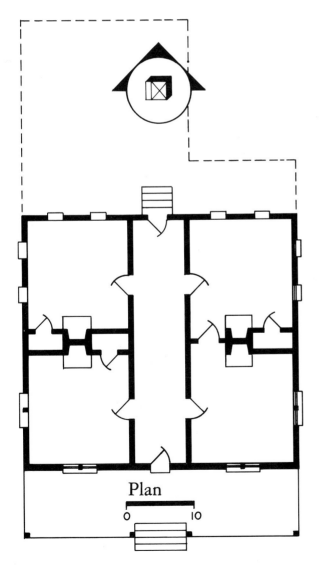

Plan

0   10

Graham House

The pyramidal-roof house type is interpreted as a variation of a formal architectural style and not a true folk-house type. It was, however, an extremely popular and widespread form, generally indicative of increased wealth. Commonly square, with a central hall, many, such as the Graham House in Henry County, Alabama, were modified and enlarged by the addition of rear appendages (Figure 4).

The brick support piers, standard joist and sill dimensions, and weatherboard attest to its late origin, probably early twentieth century. The walls are of 2 x 4 inch and 4 x 4 inch balloon framing.

Typically, the house lacks any sophisticated detail. Standard door and window measurements suggest prefabricated, rather than handmade, material. Some of the interior of the house has been whitewashed, including the hall. Baseboards and crown and corner moldings are standard mill sizes. An interesting interior distinction, indicative of twentieth-century construction, is the presence of closets. The doors and fireplace mantels show a slight colonial motif. The significance of the structure is its distinctive roof type and its symbolizing modest financial security.

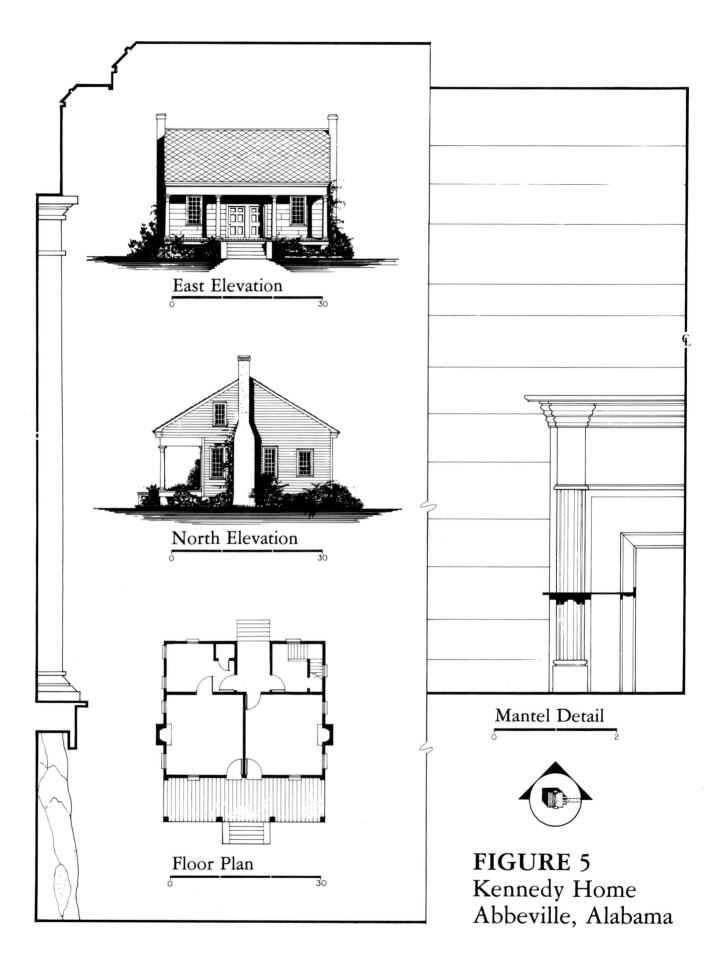

East Elevation

0   30

North Elevation

0   30

Mantel Detail

0   2

Floor Plan

0   30

FIGURE 5
Kennedy Home
Abbeville, Alabama

Kennedy Home

A fine example of the double-pen house is the Kennedy Home in Abbeville, Alabama (Figure 5). Possibly built in 1870 and owned by William Calvin Bethune, a retired Confederate colonel and Abbeville doctor, the house passed through several families until it was acquired by the Kennedys in 1885. Deeds go back only to 1877, at which time the house was transferred

Kennedy Home.
Front view.

Kennedy Home.
Window and pilaster detail.

from J. H. Simonton to his wife, F. Rosa. It is not known when or from whom the Simontons acquired the property. In 1878 Rosa Simonton sold the house to Walter K. Stokes. The Stokes family sold the property to Mrs. Mollie Kennedy in 1885. In 1974 the Kennedy heirs sold the house and property to the Henry County Board of Education. The property was once occupied by Dr. Fleming Moody, but it is not known if he ever owned the house and lot.

The house rests upon tapered stone piers. Sills and joists are of pine and vary in size from 2½ x 4 inches to approximately 3 x 7 inches. The main support sills resting upon the piers are 6½ x 7½ inches. The exterior siding is clapboard with the exception of the front, which is 5½-inch shiplap. The two chimneys are gable-end with brick laid in common bond; both are lightly plastered. An interesting detail of construction is the placement of the two separate front doors side by side, creating the illusion of a single double-door entrance. An architectural refinement is the use of modified Tuscan columns. Pilasters are used where the porch abuts the house. The columns and pilasters are possibly Greek Revival influence. The roofing is of diamond-shaped asphalt shingles, though the original was surely wooden shingles.

The interior design suggests that the house may have originated as a single pen or possibly a simple double pen. The rear rooms were added later, followed by the attic sleeping room. The interior finish work is plain. There is no wainscoting. All door and window trim is of 1 x 4½ inch pine and is flush with interior walls. Walls and ceilings are constructed of 1 x 8, 1 x 10, and 1 x 12 inch boards, mounted flush. Only the fireplaces show detailed craftsmanship. The flooring is 1 x 5¼ inch pine.

The Kennedy Home was recently purchased by the Abbeville Community Improvement Council for use as a community center. Restoration plans call for a shrubbery screen to conceal two metal classrooms at the rear of the house added after the Board of Education acquired the property. In addition, the Alabama Historical Commission nominated the Kennedy Home to the National Register of Historic Places; the nomination was approved in January 1978.

NOTES

1. I am indebted to Eugene Wilson for his willingness to share his expertise on Alabama folk houses. His book *Alabama Folk Houses* (Montgomery, Alabama: Alabama Historical Commission, 1975) is the authoritative work. A similar study does not exist for Georgia. The same types defined by Wilson are, nonetheless, typical of the section of Georgia included in this book.

2. George A. Stokes, "Lumbering in Southwest Louisiana: A Study of the Industry as a Culture-Geographic Factor" (Ph.D. dissertation, Louisiana State University, 1954).

CHAPTER TWO

Early Central-Hall Houses

CHRONOLOGICALLY LATER THAN the folk house but contemporary with the Greek Revival style (ca. 1820–1860) is a type of architecture whose prototypes stem from the Tidewater Virginia area.[1] I shall refer to houses in this style as of the early central-hall type. The most distinctive early type is the hall-and-parlor house, which is one story high and one room deep. The Wood's Home in Lumpkin, Georgia, is representative of this type, although not representative in every detail (Figure 6). The most common type of early central-hall type was the two-story I house (Figure 9). Both the hall-and-parlor and the I houses were patterned after English originals; there is clear evidence that one-story, two-room cottages and two-story, one-room-deep I houses were not uncommon in England during the American colonial period.[2] Most of these houses have gable-end external chimneys. They were originally built with asymmetrical two-room plans, but many were modified after the Georgian fashion to include a broad central hall. It is this tendency toward use of the central hall that has led me to refer to them inclusively as a type.

The two-story central-hall house is of note because it was widespread throughout the South. In general, it became representative of agrarian affluence and gentility.[3] The "average" Southern plantation home was the I house, or a modified form of I house, rather than the massive Greek Revival mansions of the relatively few wealthy landowners. Some fine examples of early central-hall houses are to be seen in the Chattahoochee Valley. The Alexander Home (Figure 8) near Eufaula, Alabama, and the William Walker-Cook-Hood House (Figure 9) near Mulberry Grove, Georgia, are typical Southern I houses. The Trammell Home (Figure 10), the Barrow Home (Figure 11), both near Lafayette, Alabama, and the Mitchell-Ferrell Home (Figure 12), in Seale, Alabama, all illustrate the Georgian influence upon the hall-and-parlor house. The type is sometimes referred to as Early Greek Revival, partially because of the small portico over the front entrance and the transoms and sidelights above and beside the front door.

Wood's Home

In Lumpkin, Georgia, a house that closely resembles the hall-and-parlor type reminiscent of houses of the Chesapeake Tidewater area is the Wood's Home (Figure 6). Originally built around 1845 by John A. Tucker, the property passed to his daughter Sallie Tucker Sale at his death. It was sold to B. K. Arthur and Sons in 1885 who in turn sold it to W. J. Matthews in 1886. J. G. Pinkston acquired the property in

Wood's Home.
Exterior view.

1889 and sold it yet again in 1890 to W. W. Wood. For the last eighty-five years the house has been a part of the Wood estate or within the family. In 1950, it was inherited from the G. Y. Harrell side of the family by Ethel and Edna Wood, sisters of Jessie Wood Harrell. In 1972, the present owner, James A. Harrell, obtained the property.

It is said that the house was built in the country and later moved into town. Legend also has it that one of the two front rooms served as a school for children of the area. The kitchen was at one time connected by an open breezeway, now enclosed, that had a well. Until recently the town's telephone operators, Edna and Ethel Wood, lived there. The house is presently unoccupied and for sale.

Architecturally, the house is a fair representative of the type built by so many early American families. The back two rooms most likely constitute a later addition to the house. Construction materials and techniques suggest a more recent date than the front portion of the home. There are both hand-hewn and sawn sills. Exterior siding is very rough 1 x 6 and 1 x 8 inch boards. There are shutters on the windows, and each has a latch for securing. The interior is in poor condition. Both the size of the wall and ceiling boards (1 x 12 inches) and the austerity of ornamentation point further to an early date for construction.

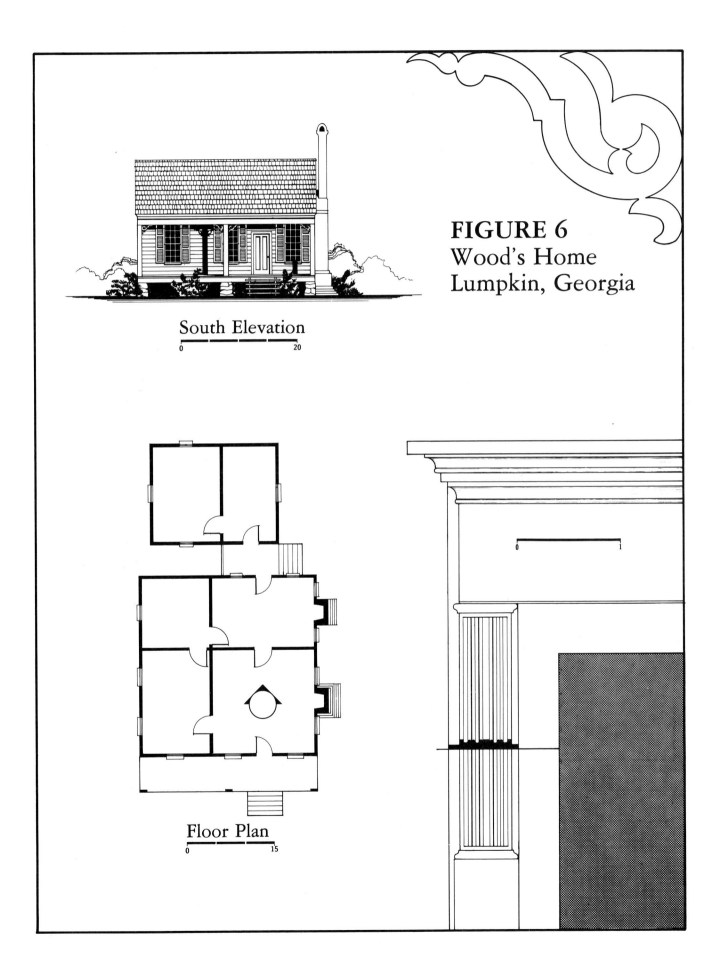

FIGURE 6
Wood's Home
Lumpkin, Georgia

South Elevation

0   20

Floor Plan

0   15

0   1

Alexander Home

Exemplifying agrarian status, the Alexander Home, near Eufaula, Alabama, is typical of an early style of plantation house once common throughout much of the South (Figure 7). The original house, built around 1837 by Ezekial Alexander, had two rooms on the first floor separated by a dogtrot, or open passage. According to Wilson, two-story frame dogtrot houses were not uncommon in Alabama. Ezekial Alexander would have been familiar with the style in the Piedmont region of Georgia where he was raised. The dogtrot of the Alexander Home was later enclosed with doors, transoms, and sidelights, adding architectural refinement to the structure.

Ezekial Alexander was a prominent local citizen; consequently, his migrations into and

Alexander Home.
Old photograph showing the house with
Victorian trim.
(Courtesy of William Cawthon.)

Alexander Home.
Front elevation.

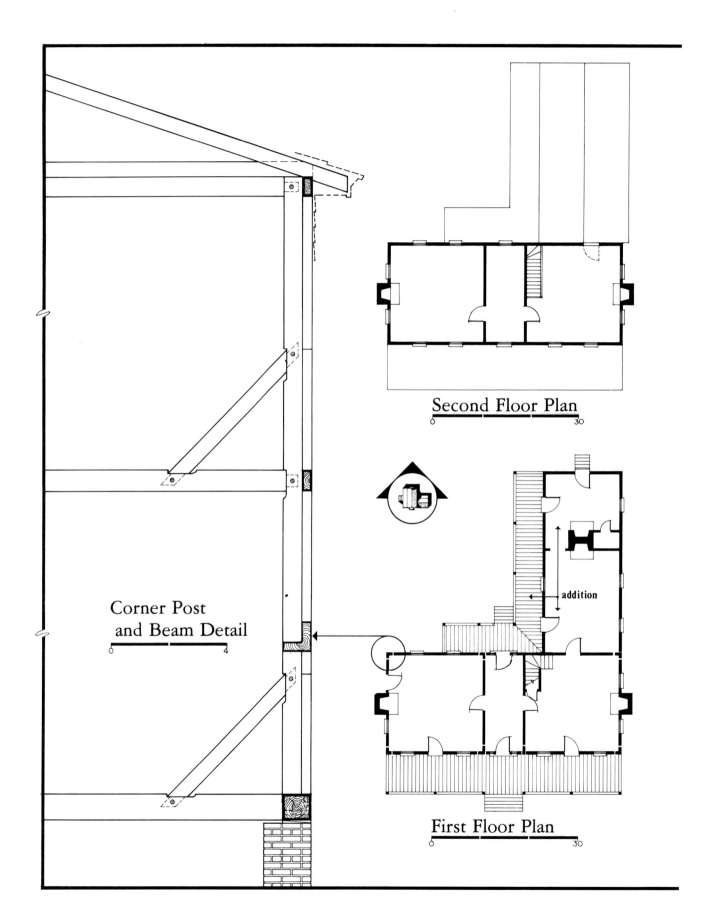

Corner Post
and Beam Detail

Second Floor Plan

First Floor Plan

addition

FIGURE 7
Alexander Home
near Eufaula, Alabama

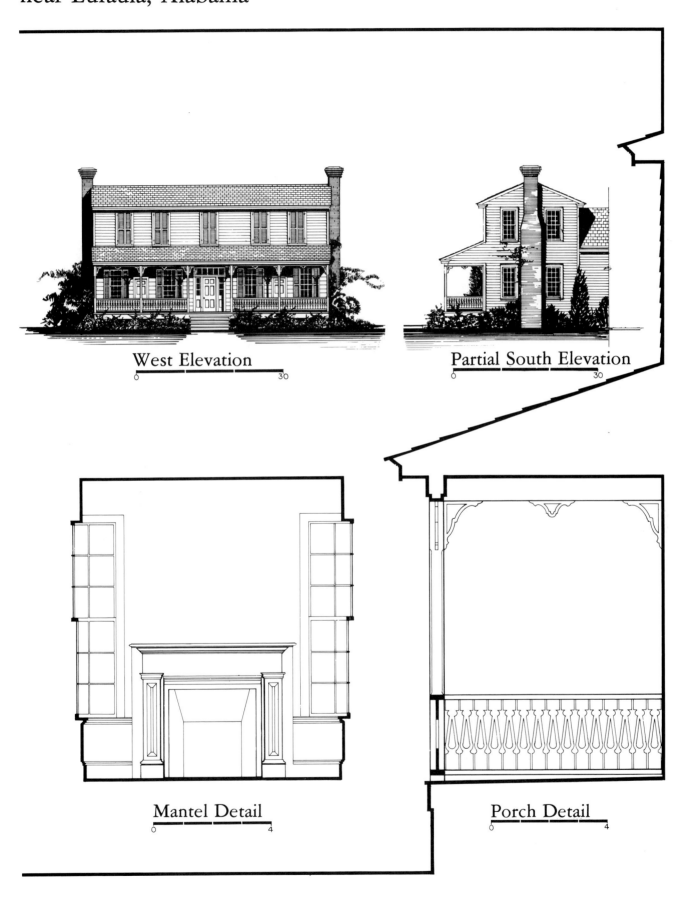

West Elevation

0   30

Partial South Elevation

0   30

Mantel Detail

0   4

Porch Detail

0   4

Alexander Home.
Detail of rear hallway door.

about Alabama and Georgia have been largely reconstructed. According to an original manuscript in the family's possession, Ezekial moved to Dale County, Alabama, in 1825, to Pike County in 1828, and to Barbour County in 1834. The construction of the house around 1837 makes it historically significant as one of the earliest residences built in east Alabama after the Creek Cession of 1832.

Moses Alexander inherited the house after his father's death in 1879. Moses is claimed to be one of postbellum Barbour County's most successful agriculturists. He was, in addition, active in politics, and legend has it that the Alexander Home was one of the social foci of the county. The historical significance of the house lies not only in its age and past status as a "great house," but also in the fact that it is of a type rarely found nowadays in the Lower Chattahoochee Valley. Until recently, the much-deteriorated Alexander Home was a reminder of a past era, a symbol of gentility and success.

The house illustrates the solid construction techniques characteristic of much of the nineteenth century. It is supported by red clay brick piers 18 to 24 inches high. Foundation sills are 12 x 12 inch hand-hewn heart pine. The corner supports are unique in that they are hand-hewn L-shaped posts. Exterior siding is 1 x 6 inch pine clapboards; the front wall is 1 x 12 inch flush siding, a common trait. The beveled posts, ornate balusters, and sawn brackets appear to be Victorian embellishments, conceivably added when the rear wing was constructed in 1882. Although no chimneys are standing, they would certainly have been of red clay brick.

Interior details are sophisticated in their simplicity. Entrance doors are six-panel Covenanter or Cross-and-Open-Bible style. Floors throughout are 1 x 6 inch tongue and groove with all walls and ceilings of 1 x 12 inch flush mount. A simple chair rail served also as a window sill. The original stairway was in the lower right chamber of the house and later moved to the central hall when it was enclosed.

The Alexander Home has been acquired by William Cawthon, Jr. Plans are to move the structure and protect it for future restoration.

Alexander Home.
Door detail.

Alexander Home.
False wainscoting. Note chair rail
and window sill are the same piece.

None of the outbuildings (Figure 8) is still standing. The reconstruction of the arrangement dates from 1905. Some of the buildings were believed to be antebellum. It is not difficult to see from the inclusiveness of the farm complex why so many average plantations were virtually self-sufficient.

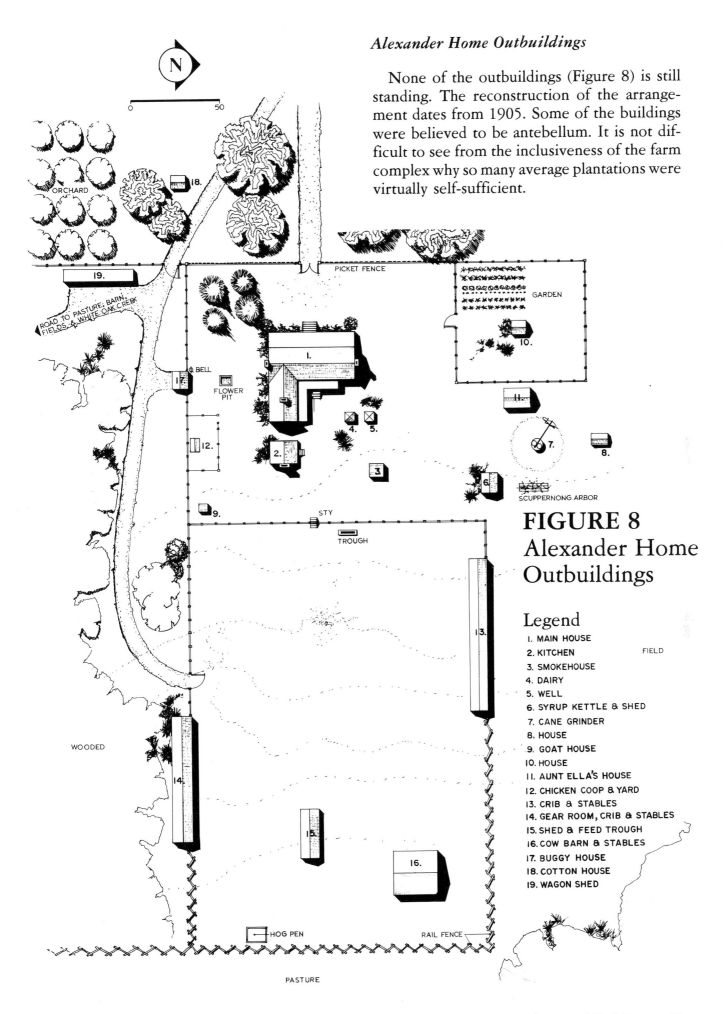

FIGURE 8
Alexander Home Outbuildings

Legend

1. MAIN HOUSE
2. KITCHEN
3. SMOKEHOUSE
4. DAIRY
5. WELL
6. SYRUP KETTLE & SHED
7. CANE GRINDER
8. HOUSE
9. GOAT HOUSE
10. HOUSE
11. AUNT ELLA'S HOUSE
12. CHICKEN COOP & YARD
13. CRIB & STABLES
14. GEAR ROOM, CRIB & STABLES
15. SHED & FEED TROUGH
16. COW BARN & STABLES
17. BUGGY HOUSE
18. COTTON HOUSE
19. WAGON SHED

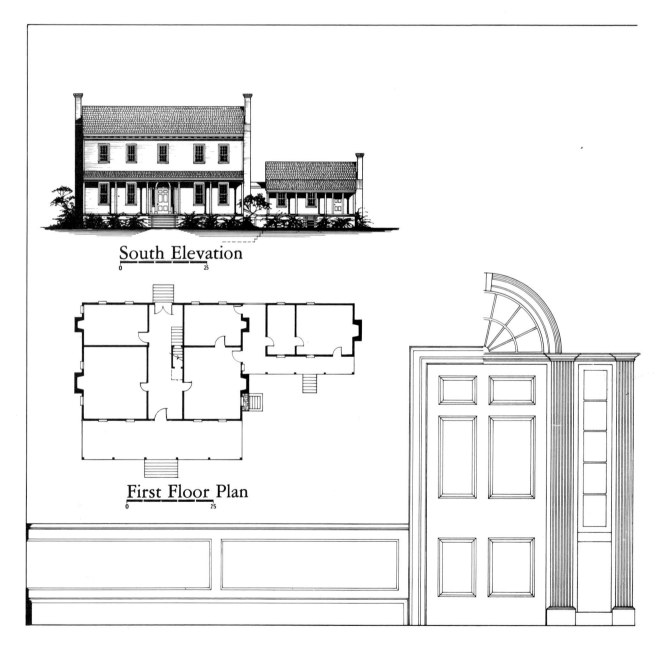

South Elevation

0 25

First Floor Plan

0 25

William Walker-Cook-Hood House

A more refined central-hall type than the Alexander Home was the William Walker-Cook-Hood House (Figure 9). Its detailed eave design, front entrance, and graceful wainscot were all indicative of an appreciation for proportion and balance. William Walker had his house at Mulberry Grove, Georgia, built before 1820, an early date for fine houses in the Lower Chattahoochee Valley. In plan, it was obviously an I house (the shed rooms at the rear and the attached wing were probably later additions). The house exhibited detail typical of the Adam style, especially the doorway with its semielliptical fanlight and flanking sidelights. Asher

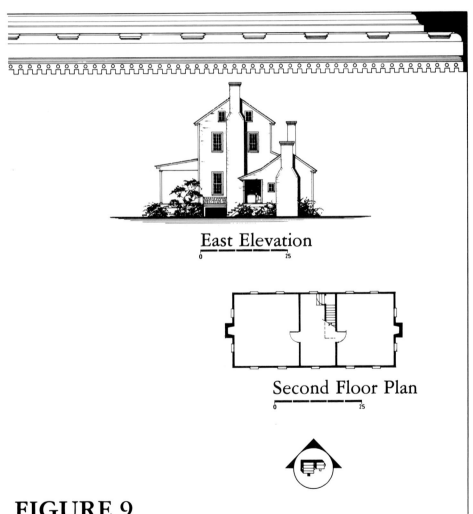

East Elevation

Second Floor Plan

FIGURE 9
William Walker-Cook-Hood House
near Mulberry Grove, Georgia

William Walker-Cook-Hood House.
Front view.

William Walker-Cook-Hood House.
Front elevation.

Benjamin included this door treatment in his pattern books.[4]

As was common for houses of the South, the structure rested upon brick piers. The exterior walls were of beaded clapboards, the exception again being that the front wall beneath the porch was flush siding. The porch was not original. Initially, the supports would have been more delicate and graceful. The eaves contained very fine detail. The chimneys were of

William Walker-Cook-Hood House. Entrance.

William Walker-Cook-Hood House.
Entrance detail.

common bond construction with an interesting diamond pattern worked in.

Interior art work was expressed in a number of features. The front door had a graceful Covenanter design, framed with wide, but delicate molding. The wainscoting and baseboards were beautifully crafted and false grained. Each large rectangle of wainscoting had an additional pattern imposed upon the surface, simulating hardwood and what might have been a burl

William Walker-Cook-Hood House.
Detail of entrance door fanlight.

William Walker-Cook-Hood House.
Chimney. Note the inlaid diamond pattern in the bonding.

William Walker-Cook-Hood House.
Detail of eave.

William Walker-Cook-Hood House.
View of foundations.

William Walker-Cook-Hood House.
Stairs.

effect. The stairway was also noteworthy. Risers were painted with a variety of colors in vertical bands. All interior trim such as doors, mantels, and cabinets had been removed before the house burned. In all likelihood, doors would have been of the Covenanter style with delicate mantels of Adamesque style. In its glory the house must truly have been an architectural gem.

The house recently burned. The last recorded owner was Mrs. Jessie Terrell Doughtie of Columbus, Georgia, a descendant of Dr. E. C. Hood.

William Walker-Cook-Hood House. Wainscoting. Note the fine workmanship in the false graining.

Trammell Home

A fine example of an early central-hall house with strong Federal overtones is the Trammell Home (Figure 10). The original owner, Captain Baxter Taylor, had the home built prior to 1833. One of the earliest homes in Chambers County, Alabama, it was used for the first County Commissioner's Court and the first Circuit Court as early as April 1833. In 1841, Mary Trammell, widow of a wealthy Revolutionary War soldier, acquired the property, passing it on to her son John upon her death in 1864. After John Trammell died, the house came into the possession of Augustus and Mary Cochran Hammond, prosperous farmers. George Washington and Ella L. Edwards Ramsey acquired the property in the 1890s. A. Zachary Ramsey inherited the property in 1944, and upon his death in 1969 it was acquired by David M. Hall, his adopted son. Recently, John T. Harris purchased the house and moved it to his plantation in Lee County. Under the guidance of Charles Weissinger, it has been restored as the overseer's home and has once again come upon good times.

A number of distinguishing features link this structure with the Federal architectural style rather than Greek Revival. At first glance the home resembles the early Greek Revival raised cottage. One of the more definitive Federal

FIGURE 10
Trammell Home
near Lafayette, Alabama

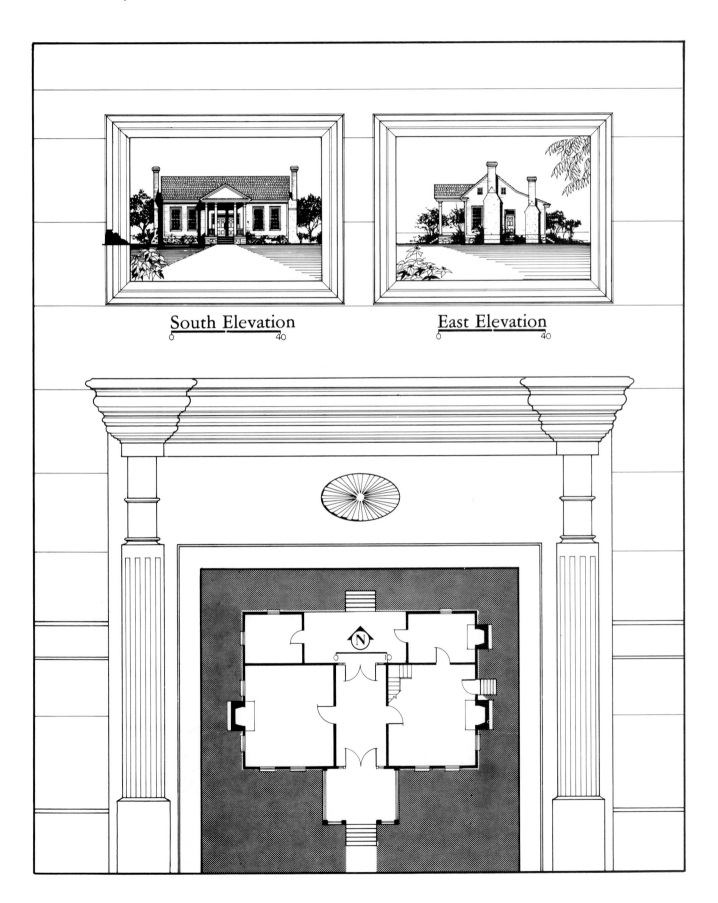

South Elevation

East Elevation

traits is the beautiful pine mantel in the Adamesque style. The central hall has double doors front and rear that virtually span the hall's entire width. Doors on the interior as well as the exterior are not so tall as one finds in the Greek Revival; they are also wider. Sidelights for the central hall doors are not brought so far down as in Greek Revival houses. Exterior details that are revealing include a small portico with light capitals on the columns and pilasters. Eave detail is plain.

Typical of the early house elsewhere in the Chattahoochee Valley, interior walls are flush siding. Interestingly, the stairs to the sleeping attic are contained within the right parlor and not in the central hall. The recessed rear porch appears to be a Southern climatic adjustment, offering shade and perhaps catching any breeze during the hot summer afternoons.

Structurally, the house differs little from other early buildings. Sills and joists are heart pine, large in dimension, mortised and tenoned, and probably hand-hewn.

Trammell Home.
Exterior view.

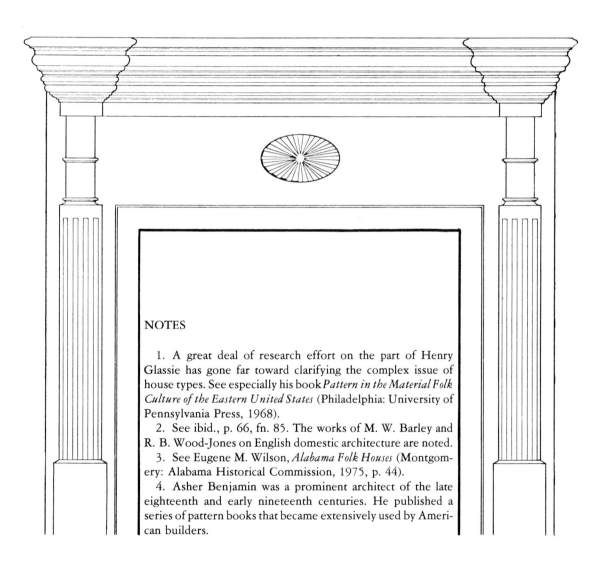

NOTES

1. A great deal of research effort on the part of Henry Glassie has gone far toward clarifying the complex issue of house types. See especially his book *Pattern in the Material Folk Culture of the Eastern United States* (Philadelphia: University of Pennsylvania Press, 1968).

2. See ibid., p. 66, fn. 85. The works of M. W. Barley and R. B. Wood-Jones on English domestic architecture are noted.

3. See Eugene M. Wilson, *Alabama Folk Houses* (Montgomery: Alabama Historical Commission, 1975, p. 44).

4. Asher Benjamin was a prominent architect of the late eighteenth and early nineteenth centuries. He published a series of pattern books that became extensively used by American builders.

CHAPTER THREE

Greek Revival Architecture

BETWEEN 1820 AND 1860 Greek Revival architecture reached its zenith in America. It was a latecomer to the South but became synonymous with wealth and plantations. Not only houses but also churches, schools, and virtually every other important structure had some classic Greek motif. More than any other architectural style, Greek Revival appears to dominate the Southern scene visually, and to the unfortunate exclusion of indigenous or other imported styles, it has become the "essence" of Southern building. It should be emphasized here that despite the fact that Greek Revival houses are some of the region's most impressive architecture, they were and are in the minority.

Symmetry is a hallmark of the Greek Revival style. Most buildings were rectangular blocks or a combination of blocks.[1] An alternate plan was the L-form. The temple-form, with a full gable-front portico and a roof ridge running from front to back, was widespread. Walls were generally smooth and roofs were of low pitch. Windows and doors were always of post and lintel construction; the arch was passé. Common ornamentation included the anthemion and the Greek fret. Smaller Greek Revival houses were often constructed without external ornamentation. Buildings were invariably painted white. All features tended to be massive though elegant and sophisticated in their simplicity.

Barrow Home

In style, the Barrow Home is characteristically Greek Revival. Like the I house, the simple plan of the early Greek Revival house became quite popular among the rural gentry and is more likely their house norm than the massive palatial residences (Figure 11). The house is near Lafayette in Chambers County, Alabama. The original owner, John Thomas Barrow, had the house constructed sometime prior to 1850. Fine examples of the same style of house are known to have been common from as early as 1845. Barrow's farm was fully operating with eighteen slaves by 1855.[2] The house remained within the family until well into the twentieth century, having often served as a tenant dwelling. Today, it stands in sad disrepair and is unoccupied.

The house is architecturally noteworthy because it is representative of a popular style, frequently referred to as the Greek Revival raised cottage. The style is characterized by a

Barrow Home.
Front view.

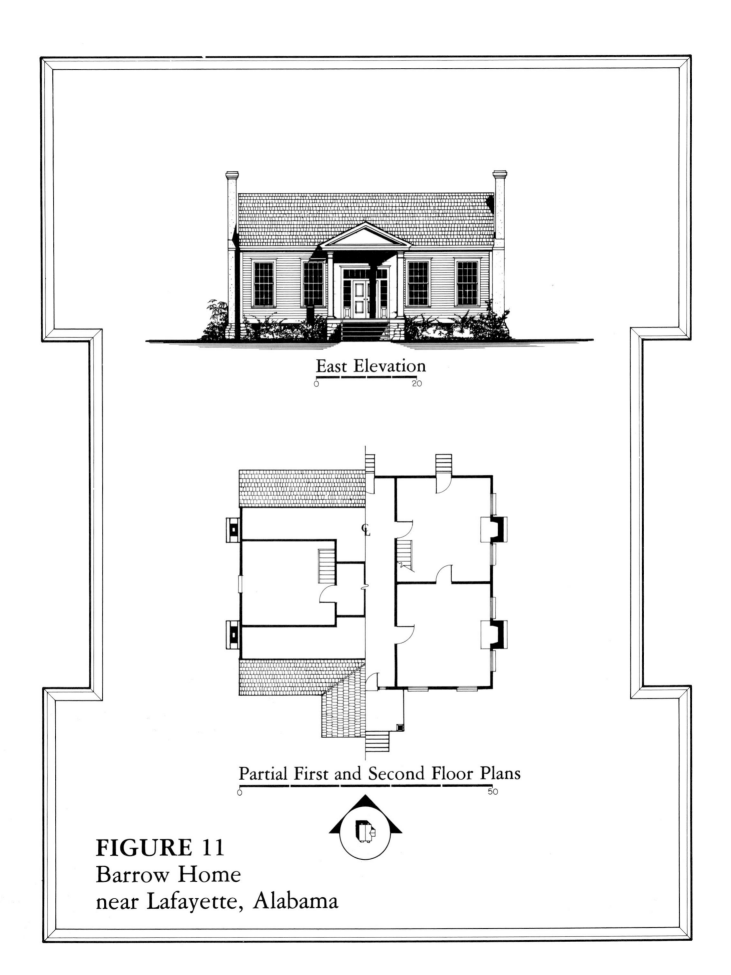

East Elevation

0   20

Partial First and Second Floor Plans

0   50

FIGURE 11
Barrow Home
near Lafayette, Alabama

wide central hall with flanking rooms. The half-story sleeping loft was common. Other definitive features include stairways to the attic situated in the rear rooms instead of in the hall, and the lack of fireplaces in the sleeping loft. Specifically, the Greek Revival motifs include the general room arrangement, the double-door entrance with rectangular transom and sidelights, and the small colonnaded portico.

The house is built off the ground on stone piers four feet high. Timbers used to construct

Barrow Home.
Interior hall and front doors.

the frame are massive, following the custom of the day, and most are hand-hewn. Inner sills 11 x 10 inches are mortised into perimeter sills 10 x 12 inches in diameter. Wall braces and studs are mortised and tenoned. The siding is clapboard except for 1 x 10½ flush siding underneath the portico.

Interior details are simple. The central hall contains a wainscot, painted dark brown. Craftsmanship is evident in the millwork around doors and windows. Ceilings and floors are of tongue and groove construction. There is no crown molding. An interesting touch of color was employed in the house: the stair risers were painted in three alternating, vertical stripes. Unfortunately, the Barrow Home is virtually beyond repair, especially sad as restored examples have proved to be comfortable contemporary dwellings and aesthetically pleasing.

Barrow Home.
Stair detail.

Mitchell-Ferrell Home

An interesting structure, the Mitchell-Ferrell Home represents a blend of architectural styles, some likely being Victorian in origin. The basic plan of the house and its overall style indicate considerable Greek Revival influence (Figure 12). Although conflicting dates exist, it is believed the house was built in Glennville, Alabama, in the 1840s by the Americus Mitchell family. The house was moved to its present site in Seale, Russell County, Alabama, by Colonel James B. Mitchell between 1867 and 1869. It is known that the Mitchell children were born in the house during the 1870s. The original architect and builder are unknown, but the house is thought to have been constructed by skilled slaves of the Mitchell family.

Mitchell-Ferrell Home.
Exterior view.

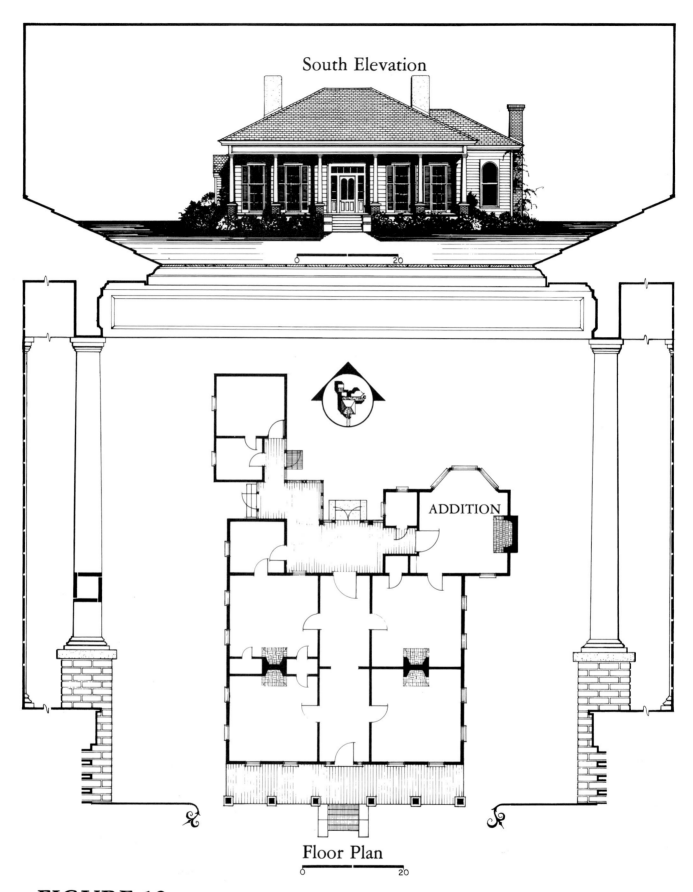

South Elevation

ADDITION

Floor Plan

FIGURE 12
Mitchell-Ferrell Home
Seale, Alabama

Mitchell-Ferrell Home.
Front view.

Mitchell-Ferrell Home.
Detail of column and porch interior.

Mitchell-Ferrell Home.
Front entrance, interior view.

Mitchell-Ferrell Home.
Fireplace detail.

It was the home of Colonel James Billingslea Mitchell, a prominent Seale attorney who became a member of the Alabama Supreme Court in 1891. Among other noted citizens who resided there were Americus Mitchell, a West Point and Tennessee Law College graduate; General William Augustus Mitchell, top graduate of West Point, class of 1902, and later professor at the academy; and the late Henry Archer Ferrell, former Russell County solicitor and member of the Alabama House of Representatives. After years of neglect, the house has been purchased and will be restored.

The house shows construction techniques common to the day, namely large-dimension sills, studs, and joists that are mortised, tenoned, and pegged. The plan is typically Greek Revival with a central hall and flanking rooms. A number of later modifications appear evident. The original structure very likely con-

sisted of four nearly equal-sized rooms divided by a central hall. A spacious front and rear veranda would have completed the scheme. The screened rear porch, possibly the kitchen wing, and the offset rear room with a bay window are surely later appendages. Bay windows, for example, are a Victorian introduction as are the arched windows. The modifications may be additions dating from the move to Seale; the late moving date strongly indicates thus. Closets, likewise, were not common in early Greek Revival houses, although not uncommon in Victorian homes. More typically Greek Revival are the porch columns. Built of wood, the square columns would have originally rested directly upon the veranda and not on brick piers. The entablature lacks a clearly defined architrave but has a pleasing beveled frieze and modest cornice treatment. The hipped roof would have originally had wooden shingles.

Cleaveland-Godwin-Nelson-Peacock House

An example of a structure predominantly Greek Revival in style, the Cleaveland-Godwin-Nelson-Peacock House has a significant Federalist transition feature, the graceful arched fanlight over the front doors (Figure 13). The history behind the house is scanty; it is certainly antebellum, having been built by the Cleaveland family. Acquired by the William T. Godwin family toward the latter part of the nineteenth century, the house later passed to the Peacock family and is presently owned by J. D. Peacock of Columbus, Georgia; the house is in Harris County, Georgia.

Built like so many of its contemporaries, the house has 12 x 12 inch hand-hewn sills and 3 x 8 inch joists. The siding is clapboard. The interior walls and ceilings are plaster over wood lath. The most distinctive feature of the house is the

Cleaveland-Godwin-Nelson-Peacock House. Exterior view of front.

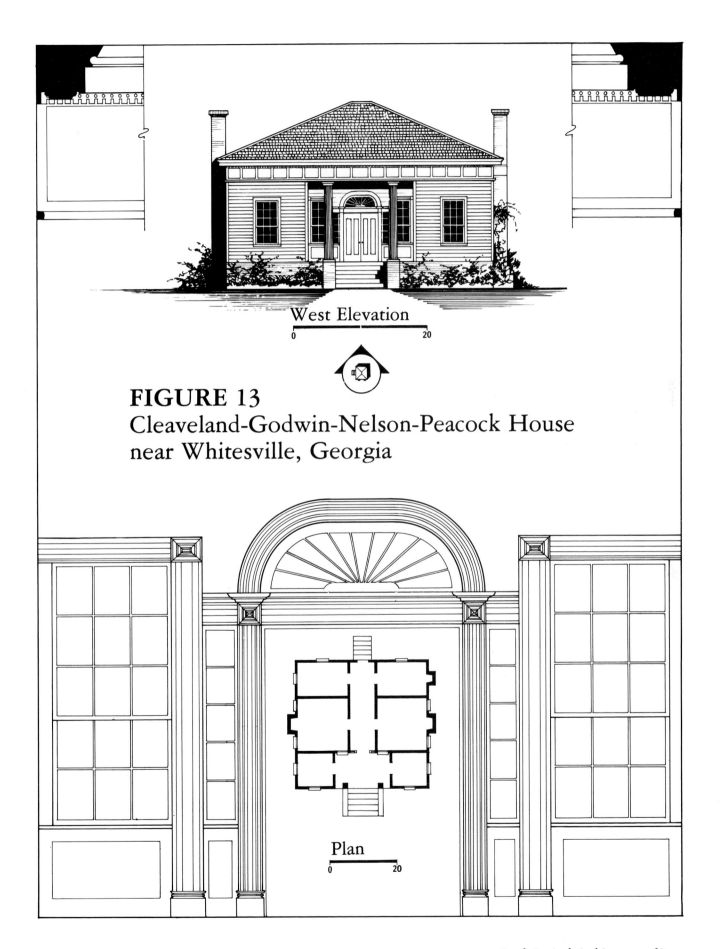

West Elevation

0   20

FIGURE 13
Cleaveland-Godwin-Nelson-Peacock House
near Whitesville, Georgia

Plan

0   20

Cleaveland-Godwin-Nelson-Peacock House.
Entrance and window detail.

Cleaveland-Godwin-Nelson-Peacock House.
Detail of column and porch interior.

recessed front entrance, different but not unknown in the area, although more commonly a feature of the rear of a house. The porch is fronted by two fluted, square Doric columns. The door is double, flanked by sidelights, and capped by a slightly flattened fanlight. Fluted molding surrounds windows and doors alike, carrying the fluted motif into the porch interior. The doors from the flanking rooms carry out the same detail. The porch walls are flush siding and have a wainscot, possibly to create an illusion of interior finishing. Immediately adjacent to the sidelights are windows that afford partial light for the parlors on each side of the narrow central hall. The front columns support in part an entablature of intricate craftsmanship. The architrave is not substantial. The denticulated frieze has well-defined triglyphs across the front only; the cornice is moderately heavy.

The interior of the house appears to have been rather plain. There is the typical wainscoting in the hall. Interior door molding does not show the same attention to detail as does the exterior. The mantels have been removed, although one remains stored underneath the house; it is relatively unadorned save for a small amount of fluting. From all indications the Cleaveland-Godwin-Nelson-Peacock House was much more elegant on the exterior than the interior.

Cleaveland-Godwin-Nelson-Peacock House. Wainscoting.

Cleaveland-Godwin-Nelson-Peacock House. Mantel.

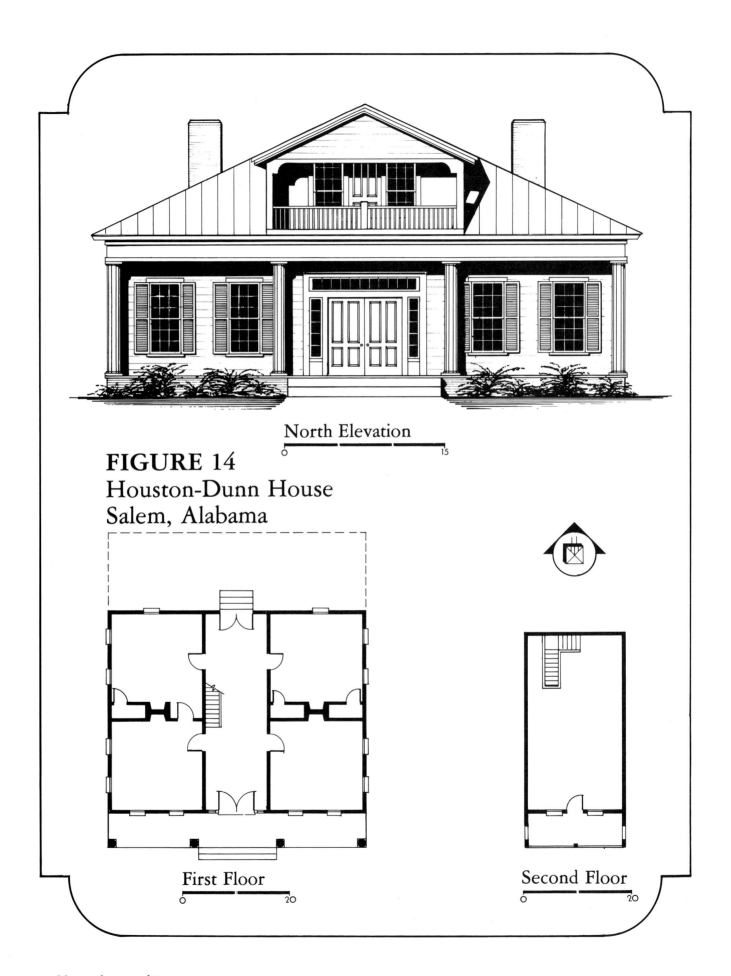

North Elevation

0   15

FIGURE 14
Houston-Dunn House
Salem, Alabama

First Floor

0   20

Second Floor

0   20

Houston-Dunn House.
Front view.

Houston-Dunn House

Another fine example of the Greek Revival is the Houston-Dunn House in Salem, Lee County, Alabama (Figure 14). The complete history of the house is not clearly worked out; records do date to the early 1880s. In October of 1882 J. C. and M. A. Phelps sold the property to Martha B. Houston. The deed describes the property as the old hotel lot. It appears that at one time Salem had three hotels; two sites have been positively identified. It is believed that this house may have been the third hotel. If so, its original owner may have been John Askew, an early proprietor in Salem. In 1885 J. W. Dunn bought the property from M. B. Houston, and in 1937 it was inherited by Miss Mary Elizabeth Dunn. Upon her recent death it came into the ownership of two of her nephews, William E. and Forrest S. Dunn. The house is believed to be one of the earliest in Salem, the town having been laid out in 1832.

The Houston-Dunn House exhibits definitive Greek Revival traits. It is square with a broad central hallway having flanking rooms. There have been additions across the back through the years. The massive supports for the house suggest an early date, perhaps the early 1840s. Sills are nearly 10 inches square and joists are about 3 x 9 inches. The columns are ten-sided and have no appreciable capitals. The exterior is clapboard except for the front, which is flush siding. The whole entablature is very plain.

Interior details are likewise plain. Two interior features are worthy of comment. The two back rooms have small closets adjacent to the fireplaces; as best as can be determined, the closets are original. A second feature is the unfinished upper room. In all likelihood the upper balcony and its entrance are a late addition. There does not appear to have been much use of the room except for storage.

The house is presently unoccupied, but work has been done by the owners to protect it from unnecessary wear. Like many of its contemporaries, the home in its prime must have been an elegant structure.

Houston-Dunn House.
Interior detail of front entrance.

Houston-Dunn House.
Stairs.

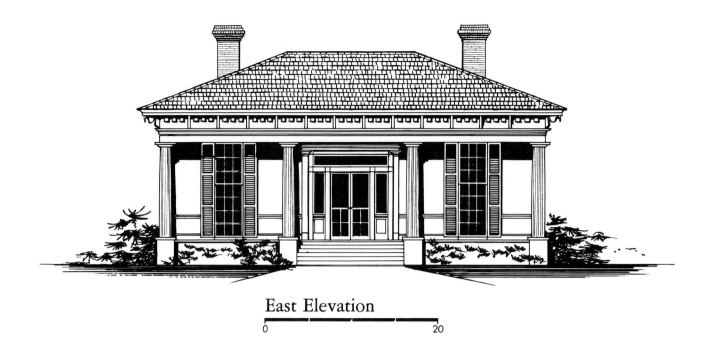

East Elevation

0   20

FIGURE 15
Neva Winston House
Auburn, Alabama

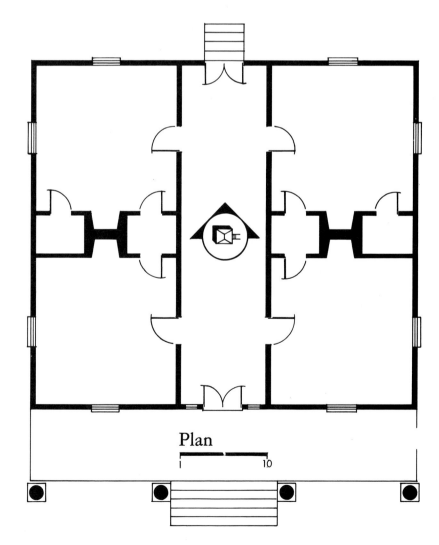

Plan

1   10

Neva Winston House

One of the finer Greek Revival structures in Auburn, Lee County, Alabama, is the Neva Winston House (Figure 15). The history is sparse indeed; the first mention of a house on the current site is dated 1886. An earlier deed dating from January 1874, transferring the property from Frank C. Dillard to Jane Nunn, makes no mention of the house. After 1886 the house was inherited by Mary A. Hurt, Jane Nunn's daughter. In 1887 the property was acquired by Mrs. S. C. Winston. Neva Winston inherited the house and lot from Mrs. S. C. Winston in November 1928.

Dating of the Neva Winston House must be largely conjectural because few records are extant. The style, craftsmanship, and plan point significantly toward an antebellum origin. For example, 2 x 8 inch joists are notched into 9½ x 9 inch hand-hewn sills. The late date of the property transaction would indicate the house was postbellum in origin. It was not unheard of to move a structure from country to town, and it is entirely conceivable that Jane Nunn had the house moved to her town lot after 1874.

The house has fine proportions and exhibits numerous features indicative of the Greek Revival. The plan is common for the style with a full-length central hall and flanking rooms. An interesting modification of the house is the presence of closets on each side of the two double fireplaces. The Neva Winston House displays classic bilateral symmetry. The interior is simple. Mantels are plain, little variation occurring among the four. Wainscoting is present in the hall. There does not appear to have been crown molding in any of the rooms.

Typical of modest Greek Revival structures, the finest display of craftsmanship is on the exterior. The windows are oversized and carry the same frame arrangement as the doors; pilasters are fluted as are the four graceful round Doric columns. Each of the pilasters has a simple, denticulated capital; the cornice over each window and door has a diamond-shaped fret. The porch front is stuccoed and wainscoted; other exterior walls are clapboard.

The entablature is heavy. The architrave, frieze, and cornice are denticulated; the architrave and cornice dentils are small, that of the frieze is considerably oversized. In addition, the frieze has a bracket detail that is tipped with an acorn motif. The bracket detail is continued around the house and supports a wide cornice with an overhang of about a foot.

The Neva Winston House is presently used as student rental property. The house is in fair condition and with moderate efforts could be restored to a perfect gem of Greek Revival architecture.

Neva Winston House.
Front View.

Neva Winston House.
Entrance and entablature detail.

Neva Winston House.
Detail of column and corner of the entablature.

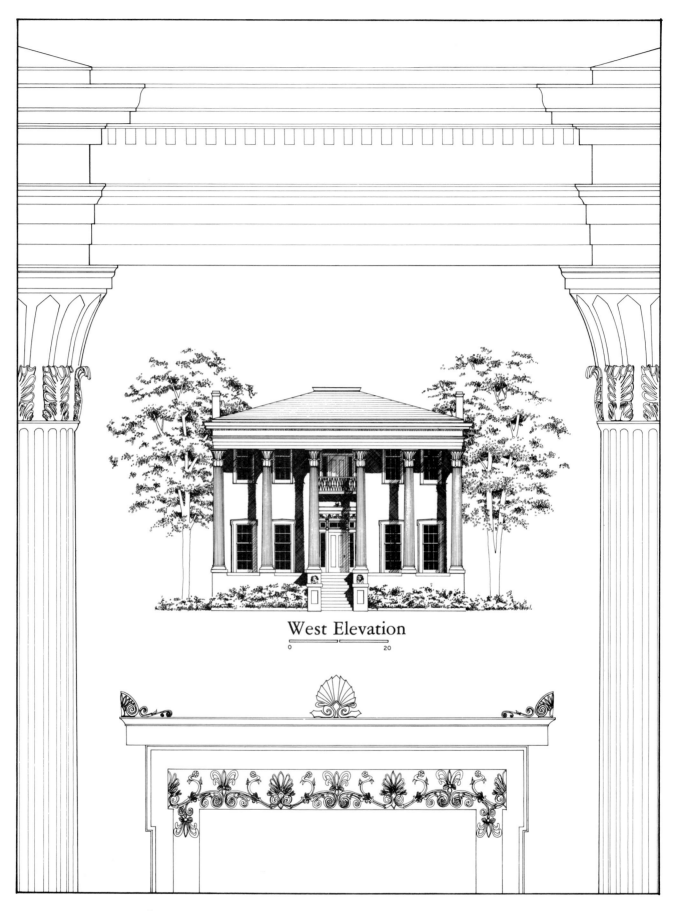

West Elevation

0   20

FIGURE 16

Hoxey Home
Columbus, Georgia

Hoxey Home

Representative of the massive Greek Revival structures built in towns or on larger plantations, the Hoxey Home is in Columbus, Muscogee County, Georgia (Figures 16, 17). It was constructed in the 1840s for Thomas Hoxey, a well-known Columbus physician. Dr. Hoxey organized the Lyceura Society in 1839, a club dedicated "to the entertainment and instruction of the people." In 1872 Augustus M. Allen purchased the home. It later came into the possession of Mrs. Emily Fitten MacDougald, a noted Georgia suffragist. The MacDougalds sold the house to the deLaunay-Worsley family of Virginia in 1899. Lloyd G. Bowers, Jr., bought the house from the Worsleys.

Conflicting reports exist as to who built the house. It is attributed to a man named Cargill and also to Stephen Button, a Philadelphia architect. The house is a two-story structure over a raised basement. Fine craftsmanship is evident throughout. Six massive Corinthian columns border the ample veranda. Patterned after "Greek Tower of the Winds" columns, they have fluted shafts; the capital has an acanthus leaf motif around its base, and the top has a lotus leaf variation. A flying balcony is over the

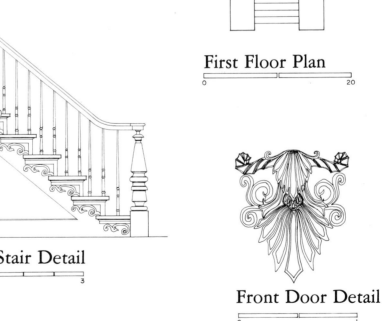

First Floor Plan

0   20

Typical Door Elevation

0   3

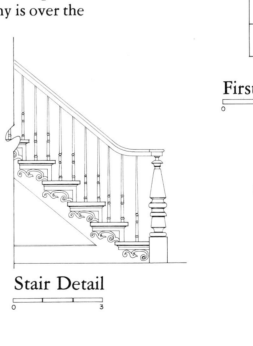

Stair Detail

0   3

Front Door Detail

0   1

FIGURE 17
Hoxey Home Detail

front entrance. The front door is ornamented with Minard Lafever's original variations. The popular Greek anthemion motif is evident. The oversized front windows are yet another distinctive feature. The house front is plastered and incised to resemble rectangular stones. The pilasters are less ornate than the columns, resembling the Doric order more than Corinthian. The local name "Lion House" refers to the placement of two sculptured lions reposing on either side of the front steps. Interestingly, one is sleeping while the other guards. The effect is as if the lion is guarding a temple. In keeping with the temple aura is the heavy entablature of the veranda. The architrave is especially heavy, the frieze shallow and plain save for small denticulation just under the moderate cornice. The overall impression is one of massiveness and simplicity.

The interior shows the same fine attention to details. The traditional plan is evident in the broad central hallway and flanking rooms. A graceful semicircular stair ascends to the second floor at the rear of the hallway. Large sliding doors separate the two large parlors on the north side of the house. A small closet, possibly a butler's pantry, connects on one side the two rooms opposite the parlors. The decoration over the hall doorways is a lotus leaf design. Interior walls are plastered and have heavy cornice treatments. A touch of mystery exists in the presence of a sealed doorway beneath the stairs. The sealed passage is rumored to have been an escape tunnel to the Chattahoochee River. Legend has it that a herd of mules was hidden here during Union occupation in 1865. Other stories relate its use as an escape route for slaves heading to the North.

Beauty, mystery, and charm are nicely combined in the house, which was placed on the National Register of Historic Places by the United States Department of the Interior on January 20, 1972. The house is for sale and unless purchased soon may be demolished.

Hoxey Home.
Exterior view.

Hoxey Home.
Note the lions for which the house is
locally named—one is sleeping while the
other is at guard.

Frost-Gray Home

An ornate example of Greek Revival architecture is the Frost-Gray Home (Figure 18). The structure is antebellum, though no precise date is known for its origin. It was built for the Frost family, which was prominent in Troup County and LaGrange, Georgia, from early times. Mr. Frost was a partner in a large mercantile enterprise, Frost, Hall, and Company.[3] The Frost home was eventually acquired by William V. Gray and occupied by that family until late in the 1950s. The house, now owned by Mr. and Mrs. Henry Tucker, has been divided into apartments.

Frost-Gray Home.
Front view.

Frost-Gray Home.
Entrance detail.

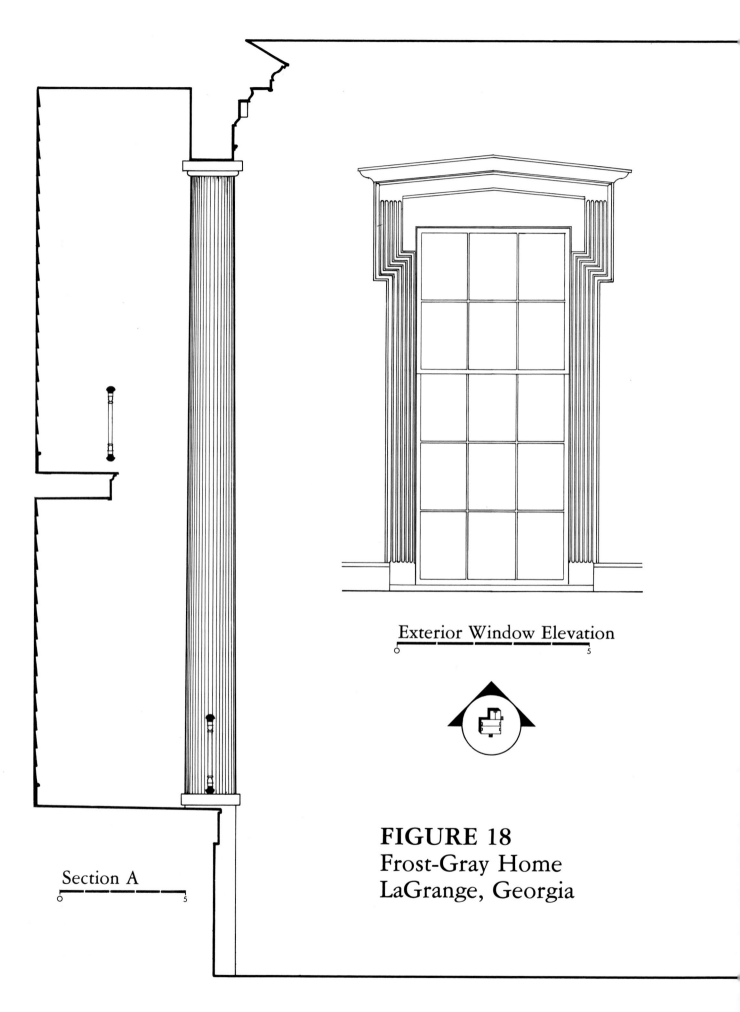

Exterior Window Elevation

0   5

Section A

0   5

FIGURE 18
Frost-Gray Home
LaGrange, Georgia

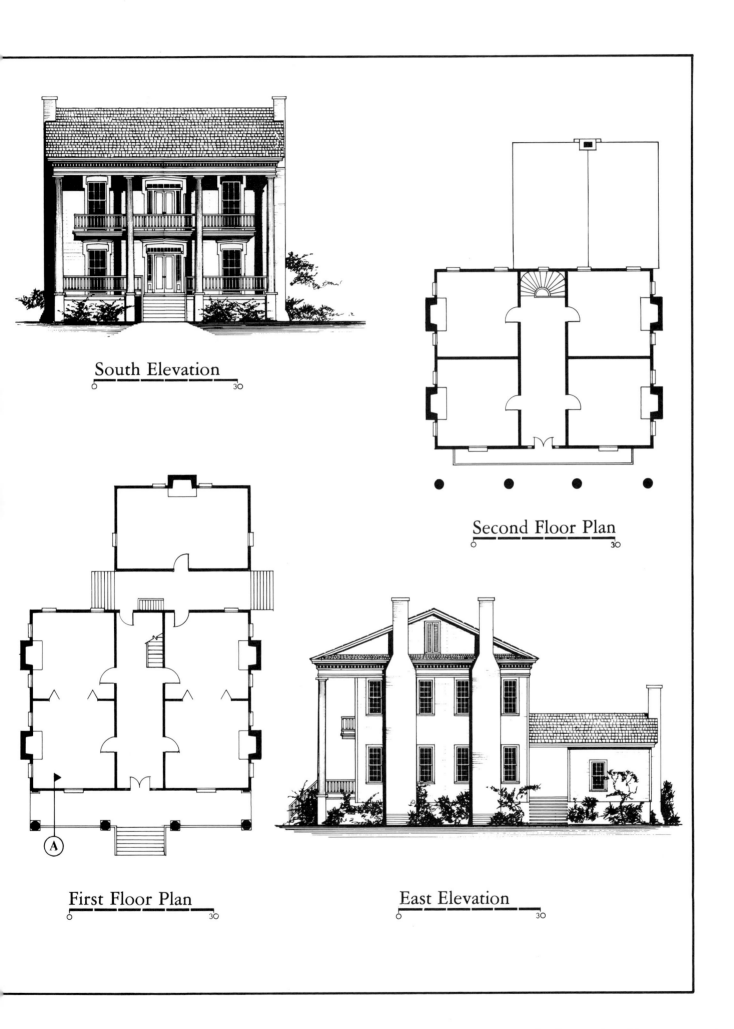

South Elevation

Second Floor Plan

First Floor Plan

East Elevation

Frost-Gray Home.
Side view.

Frost-Gray Home.
Detail of eave and gable.

The house is especially rich in detail. A spacious veranda is bordered by tall, fluted Doric columns. Fluted pilasters carry the design to the facade. A cantilevered balcony spans most of the upper veranda. Balusters for both the balcony and veranda are delicate spindles. The windows are oversized and surrounded by deep molding that is also fluted. The sidelighted and transomed doorways are done similarly. Unlike some Greek Revival houses, the front of this home is not plastered, but has clapboard siding like the other exterior walls. The double front doors are likely replacements as they are similar to catalog styles common in the late nineteenth century.[4] The entablature supported by the Doric columns is continued around the house. The architrave is shallow, the frieze moderately so. At the base of the heavy cornice is a large and deeply incised dentil.

Frost-Gray Home.
Detail of eave.

Rectangular blocks are evident on the soffit of the cornice. This same motif is repeated under the eaves of the gables.

The interior plan is referred to as a "four over four," meaning four rooms on each floor divided by a central hall. A circular stair at the end of the hall connects the two floors. The large attached kitchen still exists. Walls of the interior are plaster over wood lath, smooth, and formerly papered, though most is gone now. The massive but relatively plain mantels bear a strong resemblance to the one from the Cleaveland-Godwin-Nelson-Peacock House.

There is heavy crown molding. A wainscot effect is created in the hallway by use of a chair rail and baseboard. Especially attractive are the ceiling medallions of modified acanthus leaf, shell, and rope designs. In contrast to the more common circular medallion, these are square, modified acanthus leaf designs.

The Frost-Gray Home has remained in fairly good condition. Although its contemporary function is different from its historical one, with minor exceptions the house radiates the charm so common to these antebellum structures.

Frost-Gray Home.
Front doors.

Frost-Gray Home.
Ceiling medallion.

Frost-Gray Home.
Mantel detail.

Woolfolk Home.
Front view.

Woolfolk Home

An imposing Greek Revival structure of consummate craftsmanship, the Woolfolk Home has endured much longer than have many of its contemporaries (Figures 19, 20). The original owner, John Woolfolk, moved to Columbus from Augusta, Georgia, in the early 1830s. On April 4, 1832, the house lot was deeded by Permadus Reynolds to Woolfolk, a prosperous landowner with vast acreage. Some of his property later became the headquarters of Fort Benning Military Reservation. In 1861 Mrs. Cornelia Walker, Woolfolk's daughter, inherited the handsome house and all its furnishings, in addition to other valuables. Some years later Mrs. Walker sold the entire estate to Judge William Little; for years it was known as the "Little Place." From the Littles the house came into the possession of Mrs. Minnie L. Flournoy, the current owner. For a time the house was home to Mrs. Victoria Waddell, daughter of Dr. E. L. DeGraffenried. The house is known today as the Colonial Apartments.

A two-story house of fine proportions, the Woolfolk Home originally had an imposing colonnade around three sides. The east and west verandas were removed by Mrs. Flournoy when the house was being converted to apartments. Six exceptionally fine, fluted Doric columns line the front veranda, capped by a moderate entablature. The roof trim above the cornice is not original.

While the entablature has little work of merit, the attraction of the exterior is the exquisite detail of the front entrance and the wrought-iron balcony above it. The actual doorway is recessed between two square columns supporting an enormous cap; resembling the veranda entablature, the cap is distinguished by fine detail. The columns exhibit egg and dart molding. The same motif is carried out on the lintel about the door. The architrave of the door cap has denticulation. The frieze is plain, and the cornice has a more heavily modified version of dentils. This same modified form is found on the capitals of the smaller columns immediately adjacent to the front door. Typical of the period are the plastered front facade, the floor-length windows, and the wide casing around the windows.

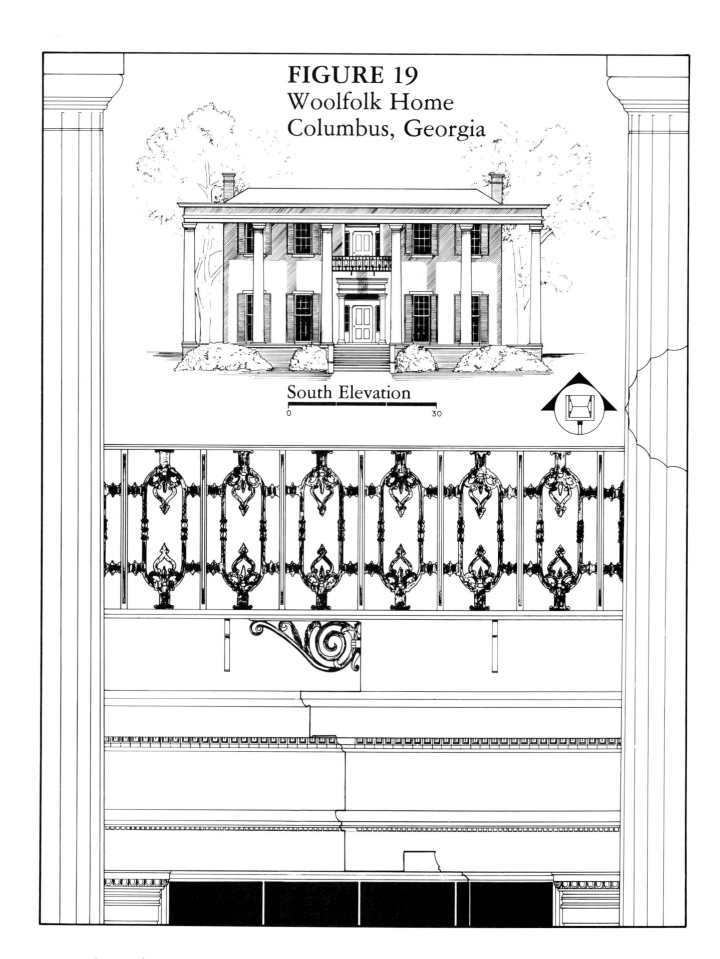

FIGURE 19
Woolfolk Home
Columbus, Georgia

South Elevation

0   30

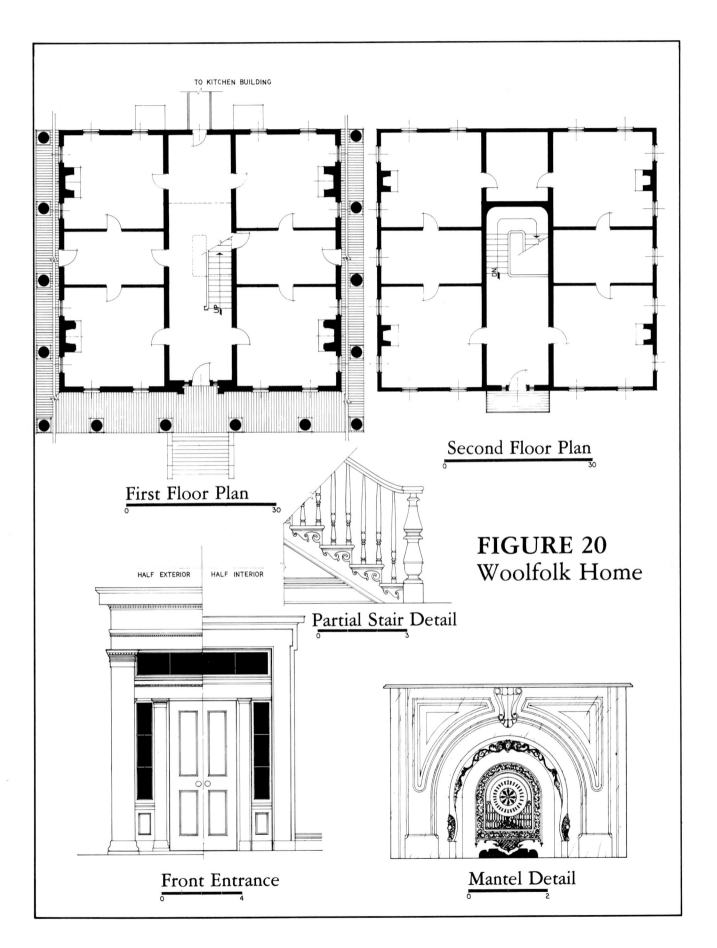

TO KITCHEN BUILDING

First Floor Plan

0   30

Second Floor Plan

0   30

HALF EXTERIOR   HALF INTERIOR

Partial Stair Detail

0   3

FIGURE 20
Woolfolk Home

Front Entrance

0   4

Mantel Detail

0   2

The interior detail is likewise typical. The wide central hall, with flanking rooms, is accented by a curving staircase of mahogany. The side of the stairs contains curled fretwork. The newel post is masterfully turned as are the balusters. Interior doors complement the exterior design, though less ornate or massive. Mantels are marble. An exceptional fire screen by J. L. Jackson of New York graces one of the first-floor mantels. Most interior trim is heavy and indicates great attention to detail. Examples are the curving baseboard on the stairs, the stair risers' fretwork, heavily molded 10 inch baseboards, and very ornate cornices in all rooms except the halls. It is said that all doorknobs in the house were once of silver. Despite the modifications for its present function, the Woolfolk Home is a testimony to the taste of its builder. The building is now vacant and rapidly beginning to deteriorate. Unless purchased soon, it will be demolished.

Woolfolk Home.
Detail of columns, entrance, and balcony.

FIGURE 21
Rutledge House
Troup County, Georgia

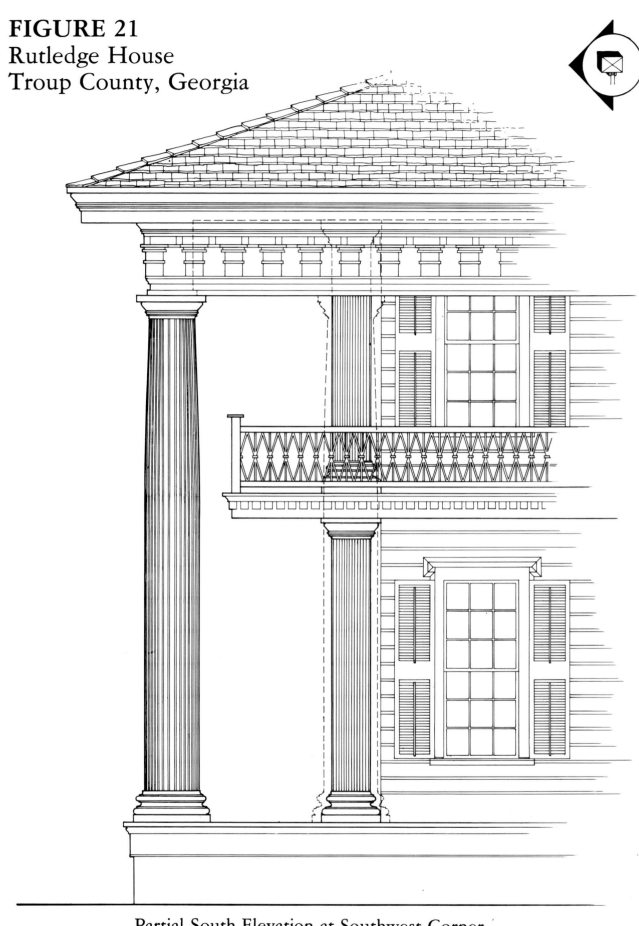

Partial South Elevation at Southwest Corner

0   15

West Elevation

0   20

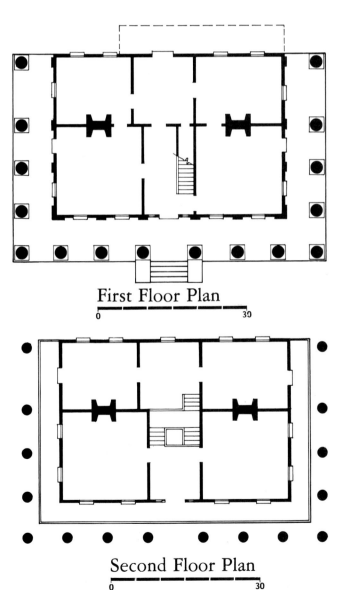

First Floor Plan

0   30

Second Floor Plan

0   30

Rutledge House

In the Gray Hill community of Troup County, Georgia, stands what has been oftentimes labeled as "one of the finest examples of Greek Revival architecture in the State," the Rutledge House (Figure 21). That it is an imposing structure of exceptional workmanship cannot be doubted. Originally completed in 1852 for Joseph Rutledge by an English architect and builder known simply as Mr. Urpe, the house is purported to have graced a plantation of 200,000 acres worked by 350 slaves. Rutledge moved to the area in the early 1830s from the vicinity of Charleston, South Carolina; he operated a carriage manufacturing business in West Point in addition to his profession as a planter. Joseph Rutledge's credentials are impressive; he was the nephew of renowned statesmen (John Rutledge was the youngest signer of the Declaration of Independence, and other Rutledges served as governors of South Carolina).

After the death of Rutledge the house was owned by Annie Jane Robertson Fleming (Mrs. M. L.) until 1908, when she sold it to the William Hogg family. It was variously owned and occupied after the Hogg family until acquired in 1948 by a retired colonel, William O. Poindexter, and his wife. The Poindexters dubbed the house "Rebel Hall," a title received with

Rutledge House.
Side view.

mixed feelings by descendants of the original owner. In 1965 the house was sold to Mr. and Mrs. William Adams. The house is currently for sale, having been purchased at an auction in 1970, by Thomas Lowe, Jr.

The Rutledge House has undergone a number of extensive changes, most at the hands of Colonel Poindexter. While attention was given to much-needed repairs, it is lamentable that much of the basic design was significantly altered. Faced on two sides by eleven imposing fluted Doric columns, the original veranda was

Rutledge House.
Front view. Note the detail of the entrance and the balcony.

balanced by a colonnaded third side, for a total of sixteen columns. The beautiful cantilevered balcony around three sides enhanced the house's appearance with the delicate and finely executed baluster screen. The original veranda was elevated some thirty inches; the present concrete floor and column piers are additions, as is the completely reworked front stoop.

A number of details worthy of mention adorn the exterior, notably the pilasters, the entablature, and the front entrance detail. The pilasters are different in that they are bold and resemble stacked columns, the balcony acting as a natural base. Each is an exact copy of the fluted Doric column supporting the entablature down to identical bases and capitals. Also different is the fact that each pilaster creates an impressive shadowed effect for each column.

The entablature is certainly one of the most ornate within the entire Lower Chattahoochee Valley. The architrave and cornice are shallow but outline a wide frieze with boldly executed triglyphs. The effect of this treatment is massiveness. The front entrances, both upper and lower, are identical in design with the sidelights sandwiched between fluted pilasters. The transom is flanked by modified Greek fretwork and capped by a lintel with heavy dentilation. The balcony also has dentils.

The plan of the house is a modified four over four. The lower central hall does not run the entire length but instead culminates in an additional room. The most celebrated feature of the interior is the "Good Morning Staircase." From a stair landing a few feet below the second level, one flight of steps leads to the two back rooms and another flight to the two front rooms. The four upper rooms are not interconnected. Tradition has it that guests are supposed to say "good morning" to each other from the balconies above the landing.

Baseboards, cornices, and door trim are heavy. Door trim and exterior window trim are identical. The original front door and all interior doors followed the "Cross and Open Bible" pattern. The mantels are of wood and marble; all eight mantels are remarkably uncluttered and chaste, yet without severity.

The house is deteriorating rapidly. Part of the rear areas have rotted from roof leakage, and there is some settling of the foundation. The house and three acres of land have recently been on the market. With proper attention the Rutledge House could once more be the elegant structure it was. It is now on the National Register.

Rutledge House.
The "Good Morning Staircase."

Rutledge House.
Mantel detail.

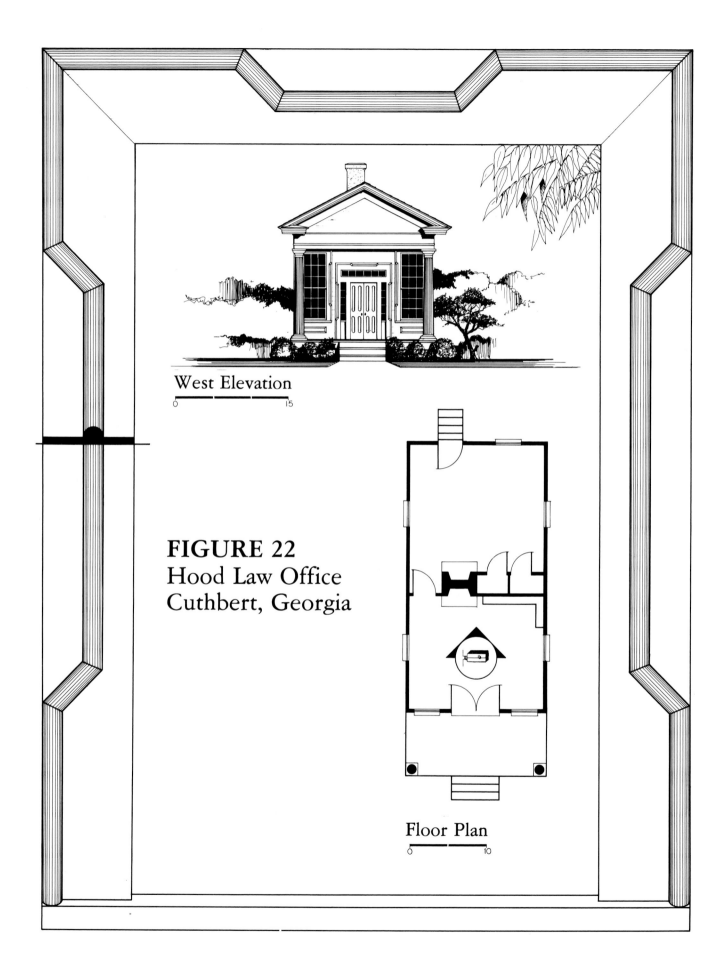

West Elevation

0   15

FIGURE 22
Hood Law Office
Cuthbert, Georgia

Floor Plan

0   10

Hood Law Office

An interesting example of the Greek Revival temple-form structure was the antebellum law office of Arthur Hood, a judge of Cuthbert, Randolph County, Georgia (Figure 22). The law office was accidently destroyed during moving in June 1976. The building had been donated by the Bobby Lovett family to the Randolph County Historical Society. While being moved to Andrew College, where it was to be restored for possible use as a chapel, the office crumbled. It is completely beyond preservation.

Despite its untimely fate, the building was important because it reflected the widespread use of the temple-form. After 1833 temple-form houses were quite common, characterized by the entrance being in a gable end, rather than on a side of the structure. The style was commonly used for churches, schools, courthouses, office buildings, and other public edifices.

The original owner, attorney Hood, came to Cuthbert in 1853. It is presumed he had the structure built; he occupied it as a law office for a number of years. Hood served in the State Convention at Milledgeville in 1860 when Georgia seceded from the Union. He was the organizing secretary of the convention and personally opposed secession. When majority rule prevailed, however, he returned to Cuthbert and enlisted in the Confederate Army. He served as a lieutenant colonel in the 2nd Georgia Cavalry. Following the war, he became judge of the Pataula Judicial Circuit. The most recent use of the building has been as a business office for Lovett Construction Company.

The law office was two rooms deep with a double-hearth fireplace. Typical of Greek Revival were the oversized windows, trabeated doorway with transom and sidelights, the fluted Doric columns, and the simple, yet graceful gable pediment. Characteristically the front exterior was of flush siding, a technique used to accentuate the shadow detail of heavy window and door casings. The Hood office windows and door were outlined by a bold relief, semicircle banding (see cross-section detail of drawing). All other siding was clapboard. The frieze of the pediment was carried back along the two sides of the building.

The interior was plain. Walls were of flush siding. The mantel was a simple, undistinguished type similar to that found in the Barrow Home. The bookshelves in the front room were probably original, considering the intended use of the building. The Cuthbert Community is poorer for its loss.

Hood Law Office.
Front view.

Hood Law Office.
Detail of front door and windows.

Hood Law Office.
Side and rear view.

Uchee Methodist Church.
Front and side view.

Uchee Methodist Church

Churches were a favorite medium for the Greek Revival temple-form, and Uchee Methodist Church in Russell County, Alabama, is representative (Figure 23). The Uchee Methodist Mission was one of the earliest religious organizations in east Alabama, having been established shortly after the territory was ceded by the Creeks. The actual date of construction is unknown, but it is reasonable to assume the structure is antebellum. Around 1837, John McTyeire was the first Methodist to settle in the former Creek lands; he is generally regarded as one of the founders of Uchee Chapel. The actual builder is credited as being L. S. Johnson.

The building shows interesting facade detail. Accented by four square columns supporting a large but plain pediment, the effect is carried to the facade with the use of matching pilasters at the edge of the porch, on either side of the two entrances and on either side of the central window. The wall is finished in such a way that each clapboard is separated by a space of approxi-

FIGURE 23
Uchee Methodist Church
Uchee, Alabama

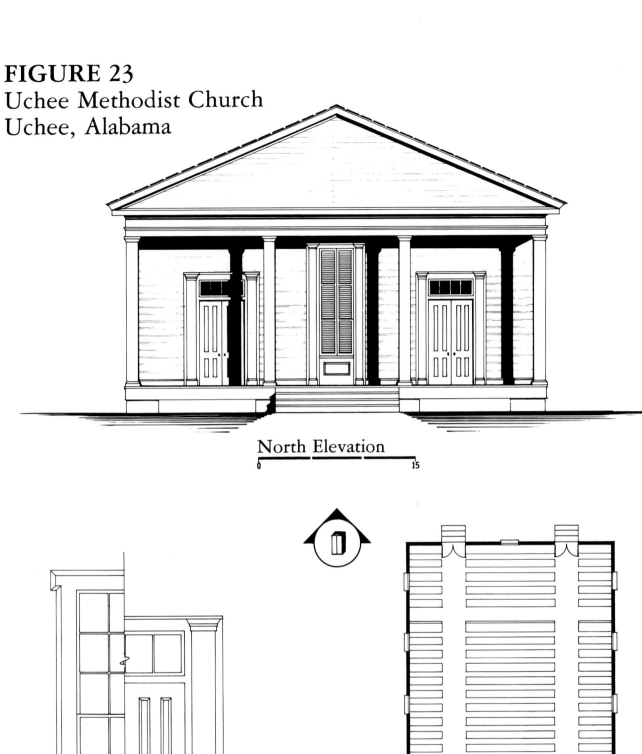

North Elevation

0   15

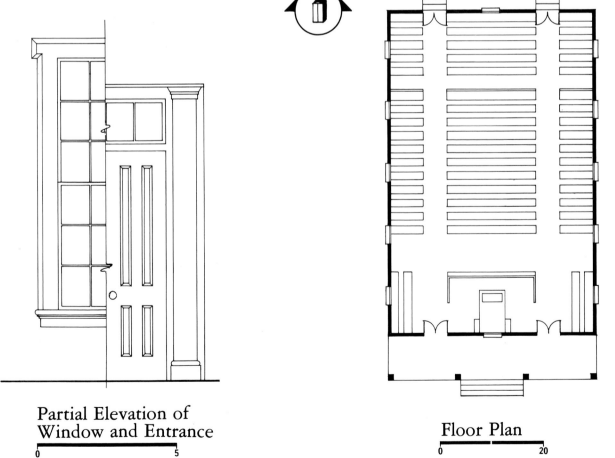

Partial Elevation of
Window and Entrance

0   5

Floor Plan

0   20

Uchee Methodist Church.
Detail of front porch.

Uchee Methodist Church.
Window and shutter detail. Note the triple shutter segments.

Uchee Methodist Church.
Rear door detail. All doors in the church are identical.

mately two inches—a horizontal board and batten effect. The entablature is not heavy, nor are the eaves particularly deep. All windows are shuttered; front and rear doors are identical in format and design.

The interior is characterized by austerity of design and ornamentation. Walls are plaster on lath; the ceiling is beaded tongue and groove, likely a later addition. The only prominent detail is the beveled window casings. The church floor plan shows the pulpit at the entrance of the church, the reverse of today's church design. Aisles lead down either side aligning the front and rear doors. A break in the pew arrangement toward the rear indicates the rear was for the use of slaves attending worship, a common arrangement in antebellum churches. The building stands today as a symbol of the early strength of the church in "civilizing" communities.

Uchee Methodist Church.
View of the podium. The altar railing is not original.

FIGURE 24
Goodhope Baptist Church
Uchee, Alabama

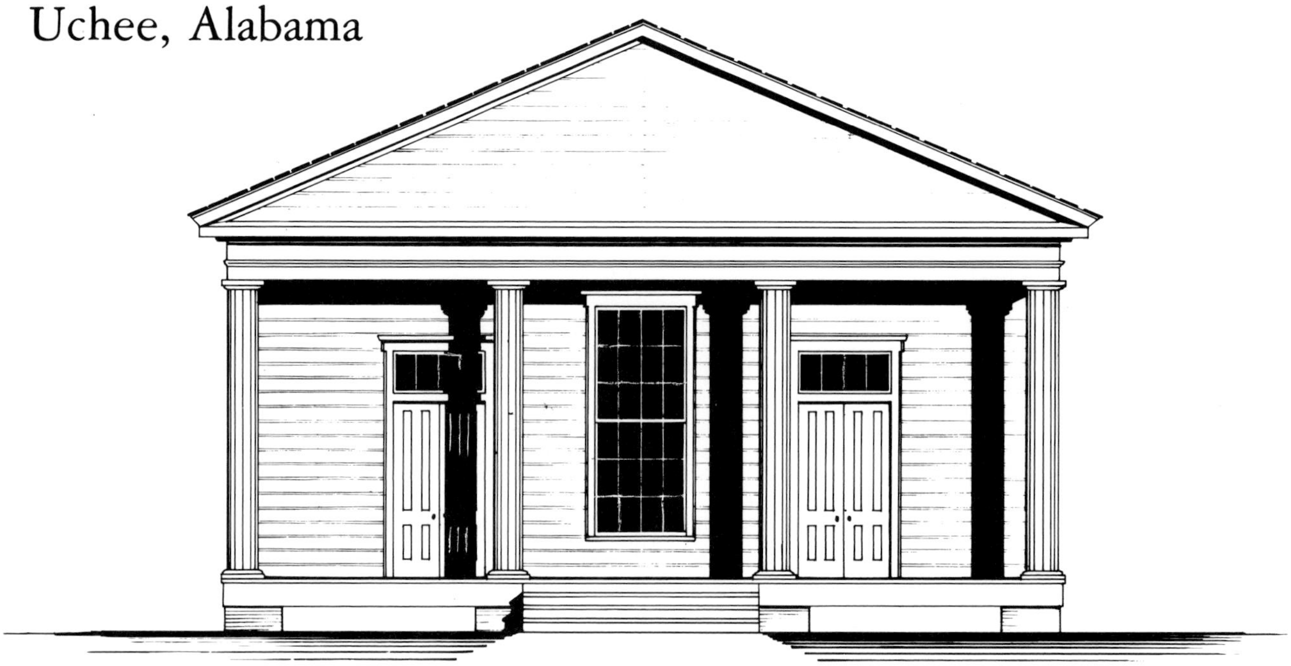

South Elevation

0   15

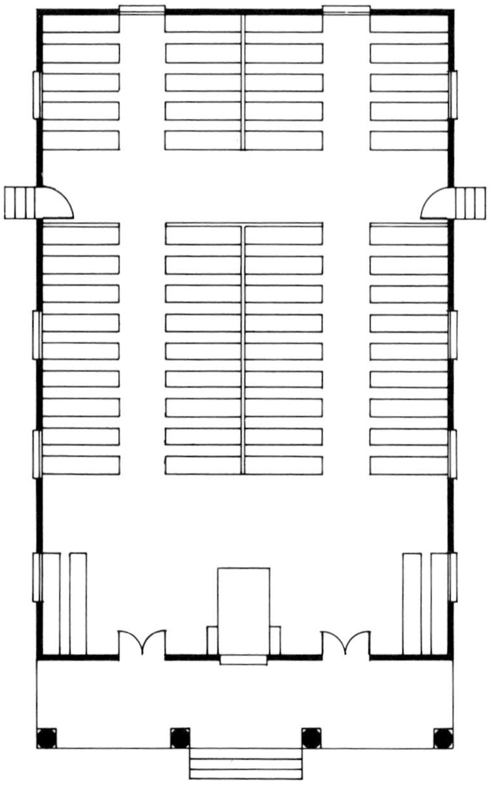

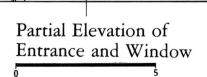

Floor Plan

0   20

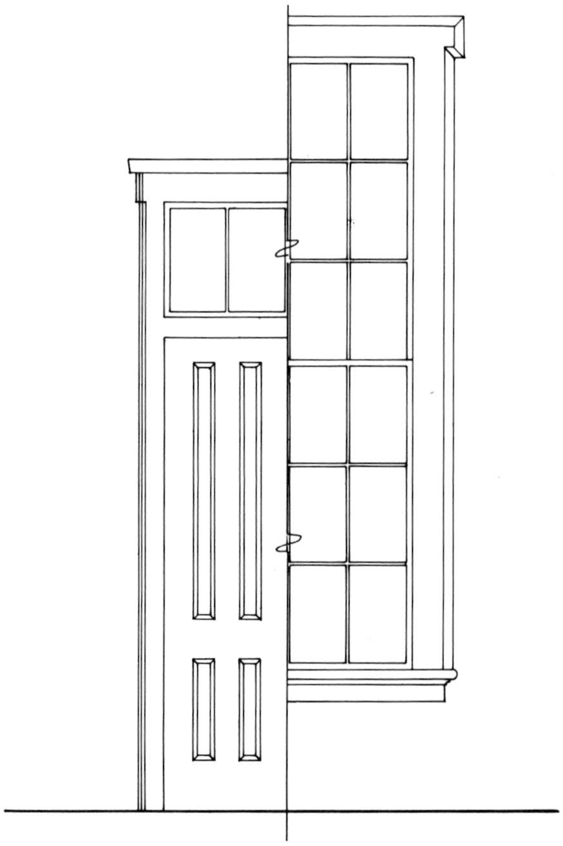

Partial Elevation of
Entrance and Window

0   5

Goodhope Baptist Church

A church that varies slightly in design from Uchee Methodist is Goodhope Baptist Church (Figure 24), also in Russell County, Alabama. The stark similarity in such a restricted community suggests that both were designed by the same architect, but this is only supposition. Fortunately, some of the original minutes of the church exist, and the architectural design of the church can be authenticated.

The land for the church was donated by F. G. Thomas, and construction was begun in July of 1859. The architect is unknown. According to

Goodhope Baptist Church.
Front and side elevation.

Goodhope Baptist Church.
Detail of pilaster and eave.

original minutes of the church: "the building is to be 40 feet by 60 feet and not less than 16 feet to the pitch of the roof. The colonnaded porch is to be 8 feet wide and have two entrances. There will be one door in each side of the slaves' 'apartment' in the rear of the church. There are to be four windows on each side and two in the rear wall, each with 24 panes 12 x 20 inches each. There are to be blinds (shutters) for each window. The pulpit platform is to be in the front between the entrances, 12 or 14 inches high, 5 feet wide, and 8 feet deep. Behind the pulpit will be a window with 12 lights per sash. All seats are to be built with solid backs. The front doors are to be folding or paneled. Side doors will be single or paneled. The walls are to be plastered and neatly finished or painted. The whole structure is to be elevated on pillars of brick."[5] New roofs were added in 1873 and 1896.

The church is a testimony to the original members in that it appears to have been constructed according to the wishes of the congregation. It is important as one of the earliest churches in lower east Alabama. Many locally prominent families were associated with the church including Jelks, Covington, Miles, Davis, Turner, Richardson, Long, and Ingram.

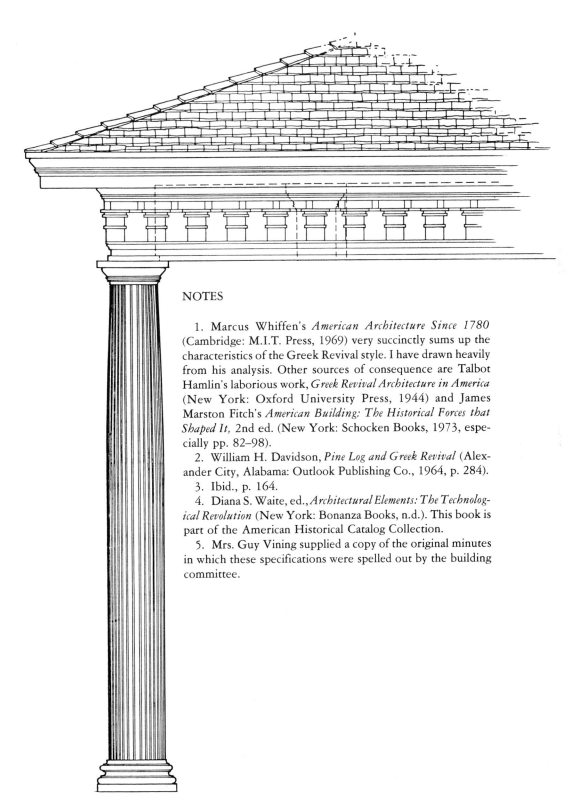

NOTES

1. Marcus Whiffen's *American Architecture Since 1780* (Cambridge: M.I.T. Press, 1969) very succinctly sums up the characteristics of the Greek Revival style. I have drawn heavily from his analysis. Other sources of consequence are Talbot Hamlin's laborious work, *Greek Revival Architecture in America* (New York: Oxford University Press, 1944) and James Marston Fitch's *American Building: The Historical Forces that Shaped It,* 2nd ed. (New York: Schocken Books, 1973, especially pp. 82–98).

2. William H. Davidson, *Pine Log and Greek Revival* (Alexander City, Alabama: Outlook Publishing Co., 1964, p. 284).

3. Ibid., p. 164.

4. Diana S. Waite, ed., *Architectural Elements: The Technological Revolution* (New York: Bonanza Books, n.d.). This book is part of the American Historical Catalog Collection.

5. Mrs. Guy Vining supplied a copy of the original minutes in which these specifications were spelled out by the building committee.

CHAPTER FOUR

Victorian Architecture

VICTORIAN ARCHITECTURE has more emotional appeal than has virtually any other style. That it was a radical style change is well established. Purists prefer to think of Victorian as an "unstyle" having no definite characteristics. This attitude is, I believe, a prime example of adverse emotional reaction to a very important period in architectural history. One of the most significant aspects of the whole Victorian era is that the style completely permeated society. Georgian, Federalist, Greek Revival, and others were the styles of the well-to-do. Any working man could, however, aspire to own a Victorian cottage or chalet. For the first time, on any significant scale, pattern books were readily available to the buying public.[1] The leader in presenting plans of Victorian houses for the general public was Andrew Jackson Downing. He published a number of books speaking against the rigidity and sterility of Greek Revival architecture and expounding the virtues of Victorian eclecticism; a man's home should reflect his taste and personality, he thought, and Victorian styles offered limitless opportunities.[2] Despite his preference for Victorian architecture, Downing always counseled good taste and disliked "frippery or the 'gingerbread' look that degrades." Downing died at the age of thirty-six in 1852; his influence was significant well into the waning years of the nineteenth century.

A key word in Victorian architecture is eclecticism. The desired end is visual effect, particularly from the outside. Antebellum Victorian structures rather closely follow revival styles, that is, they incorporate motifs and designs from the Classic, Greek, Gothic, Romanesque, and Renaissance. Following the Civil War, structures become more complex. Motifs are borrowed, combined, and reworked freely. Lancaster refers to the post–Civil War period as Picturesque Eclecticism.[3]

The Lower Chattahoochee Valley has more architectural examples from the latter nineteenth century than from early Victorian times. Two styles are especially dominant, Eastlake and Queen Anne. The Eastlake style takes its name from Charles Locke Eastlake, an English architect, and is characterized by wooden rosettes, jigsaw work in wood, shallow incising, and delicate ironwork. The Queen

Anne style is hallmarked by bay windows, elaborate chimneys, and the multiple use of stone, brick, wood, slate, and stucco on the same structure. Other Victorian styles, especially the Italianate, are to be seen, though often considerably modified.

Jennings Home

Situated in Clayton, Barbour County, Alabama, the Jennings Home is an adaptation of the Victorian Italianate style (Figure 25). While lacking the Palladian windows or offset tower characteristic of the style, the house does show the influence in the deep loggia across the front and ornate bracketed eaves.

The house was built for Dr. Richard Holland Fryer. Little is known about the history of the house. Dr. Fryer was born in South Carolina in 1819. In 1848 he married Lucinda Fenn. He died in Clayton on May 24, 1864. It is known that the house was built before his death. Currently it is part of the Jennings estate and could be restored as a charming residence.

The house has a strange assemblage of rooms. Perhaps most interesting is the presence of a central hall; the entrance, however, is offset, and one enters the house through a parlor. The stairs are also offset in such a manner that the hallway is unobstructed. Another interesting feature is that neither wing has direct access to the main body of the house. Interior

Jennings Home.
Old photograph. Note lack of cupola and the picket fence.
(Courtesy of Charles Weston.)

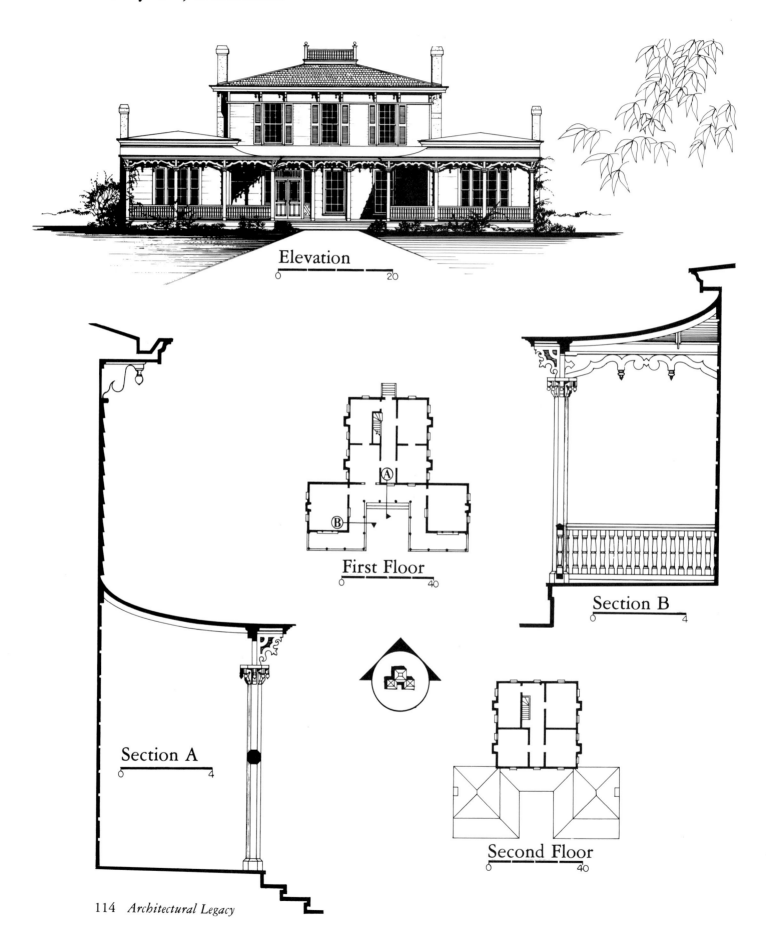

FIGURE 25
Jennings Home
Clayton, Alabama

Elevation

0   20

First Floor

0   40

Section B

0   4

Section A

0   4

Second Floor

0   40

Jennings Home.
Front view. The cupola is not original.

Jennings Home.
Rear view.

Jennings Home.
Detail of porch column and bracket. Note the old oil lamp.

Jennings Home.
Front entrance.

Jennings Home.
Interior detail of front entrance.

craftsmanship is not so evident as in some of the Greek Revival homes of the same period. Walls are plaster on lath. There is a heavy plaster cornice in the wings. Baseboards and door and window trim are heavy. The stairway has ponderous balusters and posts.

Indicative of the Victorian spirit, the outside shows more attention to detail than the interior. The eaves are graced with ornate, sawnwood brackets. The porch columns are octa-gonal, though slender, and with an unusual capital. Columns are spanned with jigsaw cutwork and drops. The entrance is surrounded by varicolored glass panes, reminiscent of the Queen Anne style. The colored glass may be a late addition. The cupola is not original, nor is it the first. The home would probably have had a wooden widow's walk or possibly cast-iron cresting. With the right kind of attention the house could be made quite attractive.

Jennings Home.
Mantel.

Jennings Home.
Mantel.

Edwards Home

An architectural exception for the rural South is the Edwards Home (Figure 26), in Opelika, Lee County, Alabama. It is in the Carpenter Gothic or gingerbread style, which became popular during Andrew J. Downing's period of influence in the 1840s. This particular style was never widely popular in the South, hence its rarity. Downing would have disdained the heavy use of gingerbread as exemplified here. Nonetheless, the house is important because its exterior is a fine example of Victorian fancy. It was probably built by John W. Edwards, a local planter and merchant, who was the son of one of Opelika's earliest residents, Loxla Edwards. The exact date of construction is not known, but it was definitely built before 1870.

The high-peaked gables are characteristic of the Gothic influence in Victorian architecture. The porch supports are not really columns, but latticelike braces with a cutwood vine motif. The heavy use of latticework, on the balconies

Edwards Home.
Front view.

FIGURE 26
Edwards Home
Opelika, Alabama

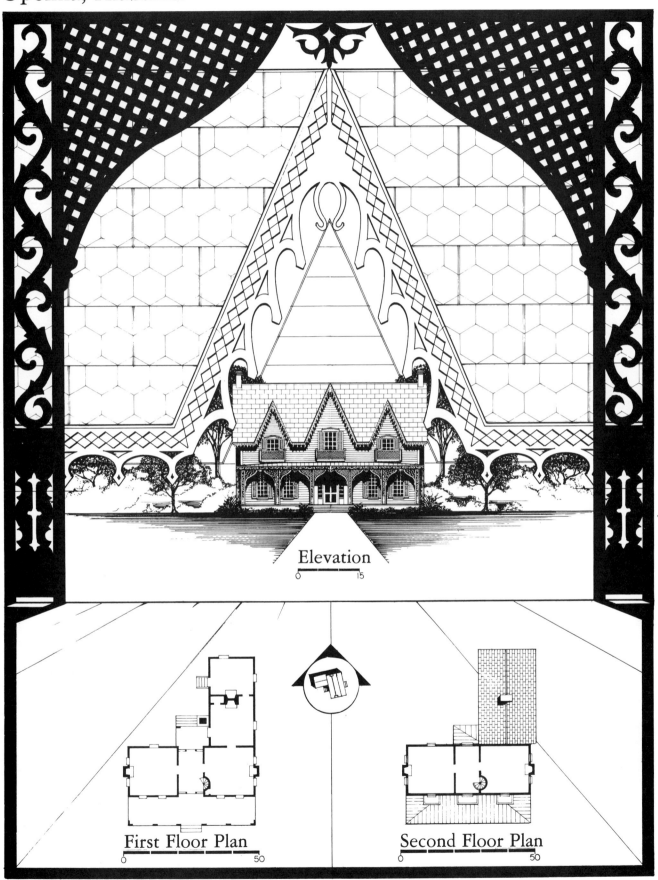

Elevation

0   15

First Floor Plan

0   50

Second Floor Plan

0   50

and spreading winglike from the porch braces, lends an Oriental or tropical atmosphere to the structure, not unknown to the Eastlake style. The iciclelike trim on the eaves is carried back on both sides of the house. Window caps, the shallow cornice, and the eaves carry a repeating diamond-shaped overlap design.

The interior of the house does not exhibit the characteristic freedom of room arrangement common to Victorian homes. Instead, there is a broad central hall, more akin to the early central-hall houses. Were it not for the gingerbread and the Gothic gables, the Edwards Home would resemble any of a number of conventional Southern houses. Except for the circular stairway it has the floor plan of a classic Southern I house. Currently the house is occupied but in sad disrepair.

Edwards Home.
Detail of gables and gingerbread.

Edwards Home.
Detail of entrance. (Photograph by Mike Culpepper.)

Edwards Home.
Mantel. (Photograph by Mike Culpepper.)

Dill House.
Front view.

Dill House.
Side view.

Dill House

One of the earliest structures of Fort Gaines, Clay County, Georgia, is the Dill House (Figures 27, 28). It is reported to have been constructed shortly after 1827 by Mr. and Mrs. John Dill; the original deed to the property dates from May 10, 1827. Dill was a military aide to General Edmund Pendleton Gaines, for whom the fort and town were named. An enterprising merchant who owned a tannery, shoe and harness business, brick kiln, cotton warehouses, and other businesses, Dill was also the first postmaster of Fort Gaines, appointed in 1825. In the 1840s he helped form a lottery that eventually failed; he died in bankruptcy in 1849.

The earliest courthouse records on the sale of the Dill property begin in 1859. The house changed hands many times. The following have

Dill House.
Detail of wrought-iron fence.

FIGURE 27
Dill House
Fort Gaines, Georgia

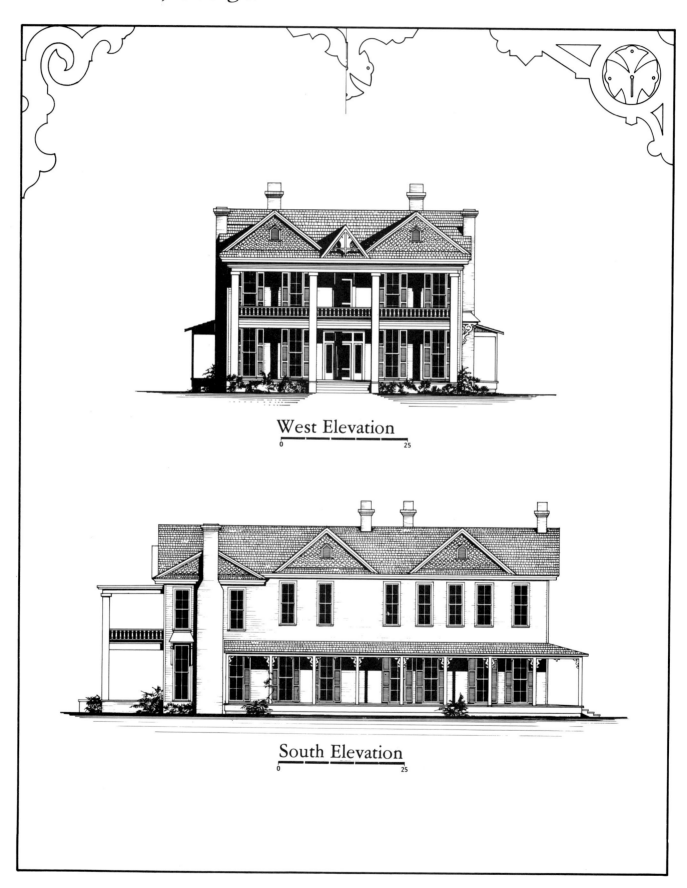

West Elevation

0   25

South Elevation

0   25

FIGURE 28
Dill House

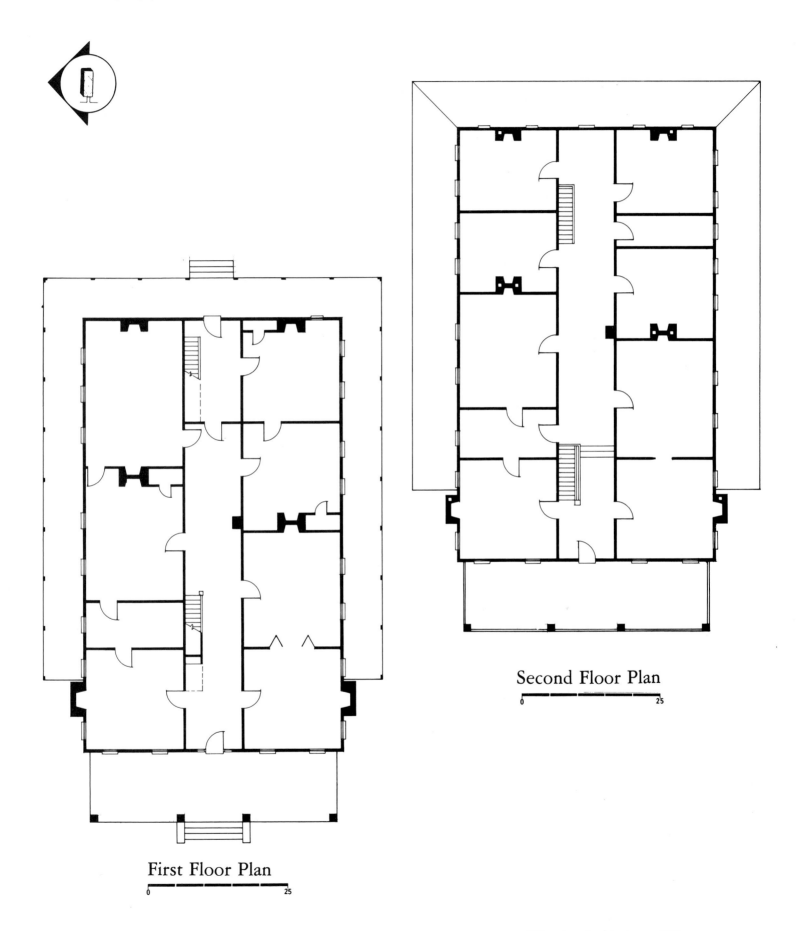

First Floor Plan

0 — — — — 25

Second Floor Plan

0 — — — 25

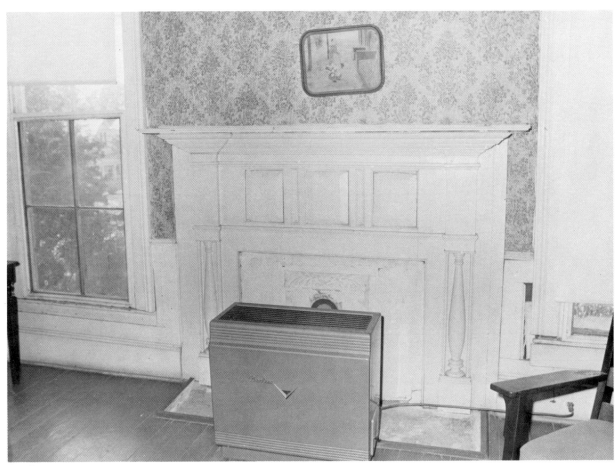

Dill House.
Upper story mantel.

Dill House.
Detail of interior gingerbread.

all owned the house at various times: Douglas MacDougal, G. G. Tuttle, G. W. Parker, J. P. H. Brown, J. G. Webb, D. C. Adams, W. A .McAllister, J. R. Simpson, A. F. King, Mrs. C. H. Puckett, Mrs. W. A. McAllister, M. E. Peterson, City of Fort Gaines, and Jim Waters. Mr. Waters plans to restore the house.

Exactly what architectural style the Dill House most incorporates is difficult to pinpoint. The basic shape hints at the Greek Revival temple-form; the many gables strongly indicate Victorian influence. It is possible that the 1827 construction date·is too early. Most of the interior detail is definitely Victorian. The central hallway and massive veranda columns are evidence of a Greek Revival influence, as is the orderly room arrangement. The size of the structure indicates it was intended for use other than as a home. The Dills had only one child, who died in infancy. For decades the house functioned as a hotel, most likely its original intended use.

Victorian influence is dominant on the interior. Transoms above doors, gingerbread spans in the hallways, milled casings and baseboards, Victorian mantels, and brass oil sconces are but a few features. In addition, the scrollwork brackets on the porches, the heavy chimney caps, and the Gothic-style exhaust windows in the attic are further Victorian indications.

Dill House.
Gas lamp.

FIGURE 29
Sikes-George House
Iron City, Georgia

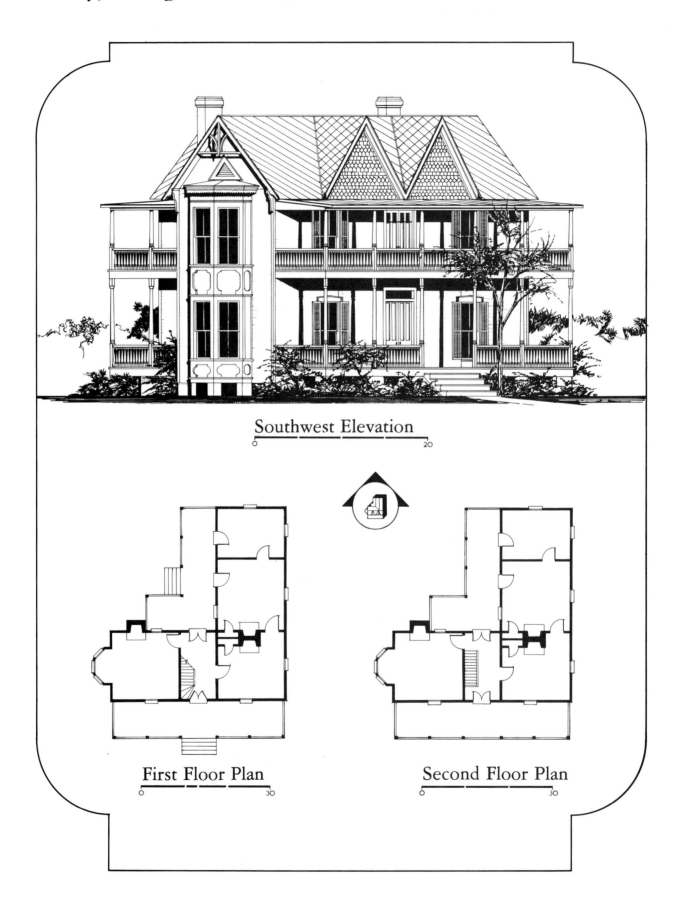

Southwest Elevation
0   20

First Floor Plan
0   30

Second Floor Plan
0   30

Sikes-George House.
Front view.

Sikes-George House

An example of a Victorian structure typical of the architectural pattern books of the era is the Sikes-George House (Figure 29). It is assumed that the house was built for Dr. James Allen Brewster Sikes. An approximate date based upon the architectural motifs would indicate the latter quarter of the nineteenth century.

Dr. Sikes built his home in Iron City, Seminole County, Georgia, formerly the

Sikes-George House.
Detail of gable fretwork.

Sikes-George House.
Front and side view.
Note that the original
upper and lower
porches are gone.

Sikes-George House.
Stair detail.

Sharp-Hagan community. J. A. B. Sikes was one of five children of Jessie S. and Martha Jane McDowell Sikes who migrated to the United States from Scotland. James was born in January 1854 and died in September 1917. He was a well-known doctor and reputed to be one of the wealthiest men in Decatur County. His estate went to his three sisters, Mrs. Sarah Sikes Chason, Mrs. Sabrina Sikes George, and Mrs. Martha Jane Sikes Barber. The house was left to Sabrina George and has since come into the possession of Charley G. George.

The house is a primitive example of Queen Anne style. The extensive porches, bay windows, high pitched gables, and heavy chimney caps are identifying features. The house, unfortunately, does not indicate that Dr. Sikes lavished any of his wealth upon his domicile. The gable fretwork is poorly worked. The verandas have been removed, and significant alterations are apparent. The interior is equally undistinguished. The newel post of the stair is surely a catalog order item, as is likely the floral motif along the side of the risers. Mantels are shallow and austere. The bath is interesting in that it still contains the old shower apparatus, an item difficult to come by in restoration work. With the proper attention and patience, the Sikes-George House might be made a pleasant Victorian home.

Sikes-George House.
Mantel.

Sikes-George House.
Bathroom. Note the old shower ring.

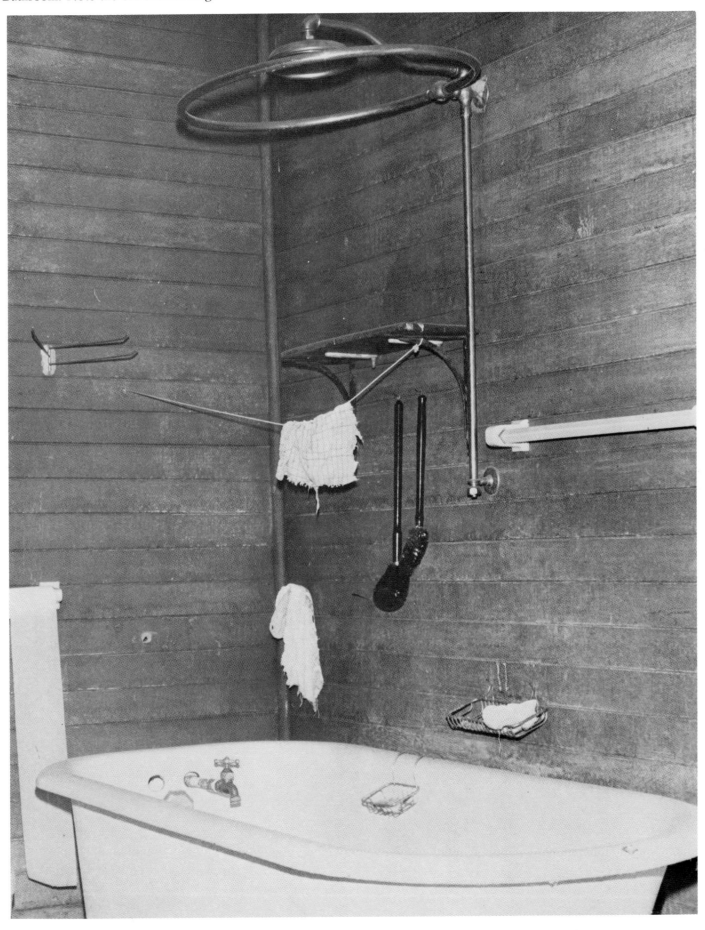

Dowling-Holman Home.
Front entrance.

Dowling-Holman Home

An excellent representative of the Queen Anne style, the Dowling-Holman Home (Figure 30), is in Ozark, Dale County, Alabama. The original designer and owner was Bascom Dowling. The contractor may have been a Mr. Marley, a partner of James E. Fussell. The house was built in the early 1890s and was acquired around 1900 by Y. Allen and Ethel B. Holman. It has essentially remained in the Holman family since the turn of the century. Around 1971 the Henry B. Steagall estate acquired the property. It is presently owned by Mrs. Margaret Steagall Holman.

The original owner, Bascom Dowling, was the son of the first Methodist minister of Dale

Dowling-Holman Home.
North elevation. The west wing is a late addition.

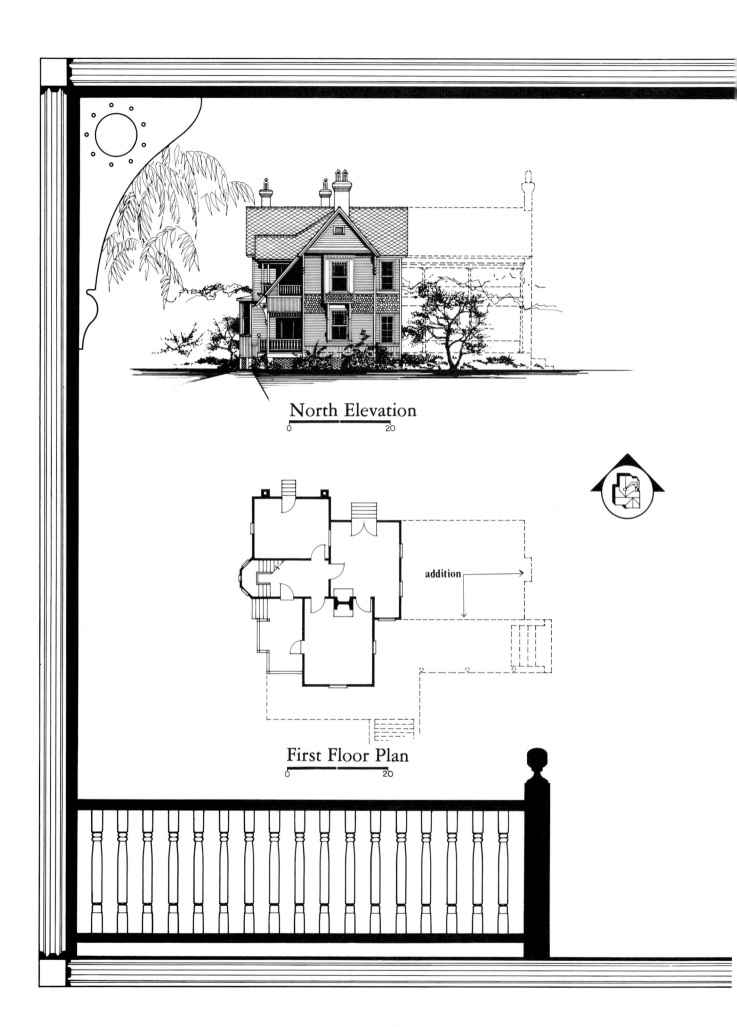

North Elevation

0   20

addition

First Floor Plan

0   20

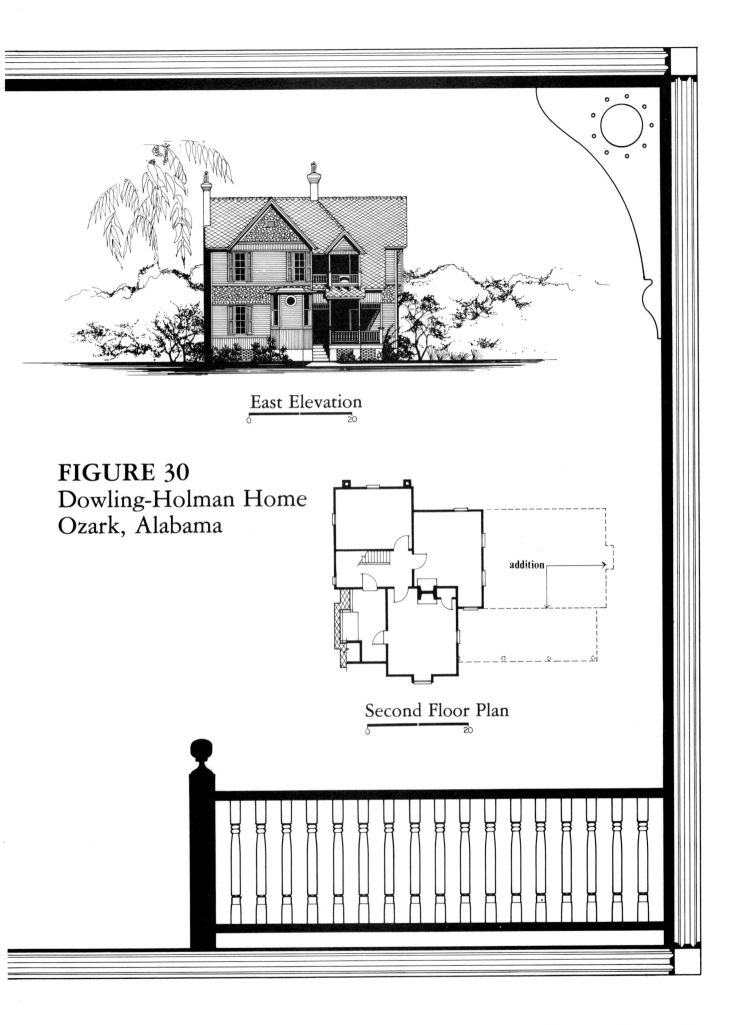

East Elevation

0   20

FIGURE 30
Dowling-Holman Home
Ozark, Alabama

addition

Second Floor Plan

0   20

Dowling-Holman Home.
Bracket details.

Dowling-Holman Home.
Porch column detail.

Dowling-Holman Home.
Interior detail of the front entrance.

Dowling-Holman Home.
Mantel.

County. Under the Holmans the house developed a reputation as a social center. Mrs. Y. A. Holman was an active member of the Study Club, Ozark's oldest club for women. The house was frequently used for entertaining and lodging visiting dignitaries.

Architecturally the house exhibits classic Queen Anne features. Especially noticeable is the bay window that forms a stair landing in the foyer. Banding is another distinct trait. Vertical siding along the base of the house is followed by horizontal, narrow, drop siding to the window cap, which in turn is topped by a band of wooden shingles to the sill of second-floor windows. Another layer of horizontal siding is capped by vertical siding. The gables are variable, some being of shingles and others of horizontal siding. The effect is crispness of detail. In addition, the chimneys exhibit elaborate caps reminiscent of medieval architecture. Other medieval aspects include the oriel window on the second floor of the north elevation and the small colored panes of glass outlining the upper sash. The porch balusters are finely turned as is other incidental spool trim. The brackets have a simple geometric design.

The original floor plan included three rooms up and down with a stair foyer. A large wing was added on the west a number of years ago. Although the house is in poor condition, features such as the heavy casing around doors and windows, the sturdy mantel, and coal-furnace grates indicate that the house at one time was a Victorian showplace.

Coleman-Vickers Home

The Queen Anne-Eastlake Victorian style is nicely exemplified by the Coleman-Vickers Home (Figure 31), in Bainbridge, Decatur County, Georgia. The house was built between 1898 and 1900 for George O. Smith. In late October 1900, Smith sold the house to Mrs. Beulah H. Allen, and she in turn sold the property in 1918 to the Colemans, who had been living in the home for a number of years. R. B. Coleman was manager of the Georgia Pine

Coleman-Vickers Home.
Old photograph. Note original porch steps.
Courtesy of Mrs. Victoria Custer.

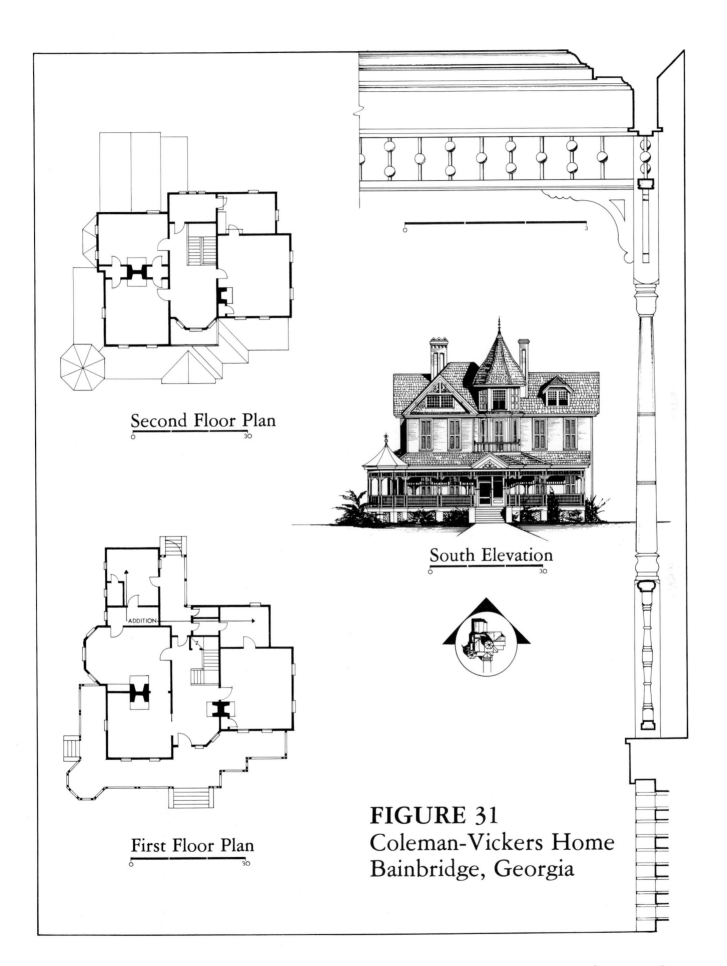

Second Floor Plan

First Floor Plan

South Elevation

FIGURE 31
Coleman-Vickers Home
Bainbridge, Georgia

Railroad, which eventually became the present Seaboard Coast Line. The Coleman's daughter was married to E. F. Vickers, president of the Citizens Bank and Trust Company, and she inherited the home. The house was later inherited by Robert Bruce Coleman, Jr., only brother of Mrs. Vickers and a prominent theater critic for several New York City newspapers. His widow, Ingrid H. Coleman, gave the

Coleman-Vickers Home.
Elevation.

house to the Decatur County Historical Society. The Society is presently raising funds to restore the house as a cultural and educational center.

Typical of period construction, the house rests on brick piers bridged by wooden lattices. Exterior siding is of pine clapboards. The chimneys have bold designs in paneled and molded brick. Another Queen Anne feature is the

Coleman-Vickers Home.
Porch gable.

Coleman-Vickers Home.
Porch trim detail.

Coleman-Vickers Home.
Interior gingerbread.

small, colored glass panes in the attic, dormer, and tower windows. Eastlake influence appears in the spool work, posts, and balusters of the porch. An ornate cast-iron fence adds a final touch of elegance to the exterior.

The use of bay windows and a freedom of room arrangement characterize the interior. While the floor plan may seem cluttered, the loose array of rooms is a dominant feature of Victorian houses. The fireplace in the foyer is an interesting variation, a hint of medieval architecture so common in some Queen Anne structures. The Eastlake style of the porch is carried throughout the interior via elaborately turned newel posts, balusters, and spindles. The porch spool work is repeated in the hallway span of gingerbread. The interior trim is very similar to that of the Dowling-Holman Home. Fortunately, the Coleman-Vickers Home has fared better than some of its contemporaries.

Coleman-Vickers Home.
Wrought-iron entrance gate.

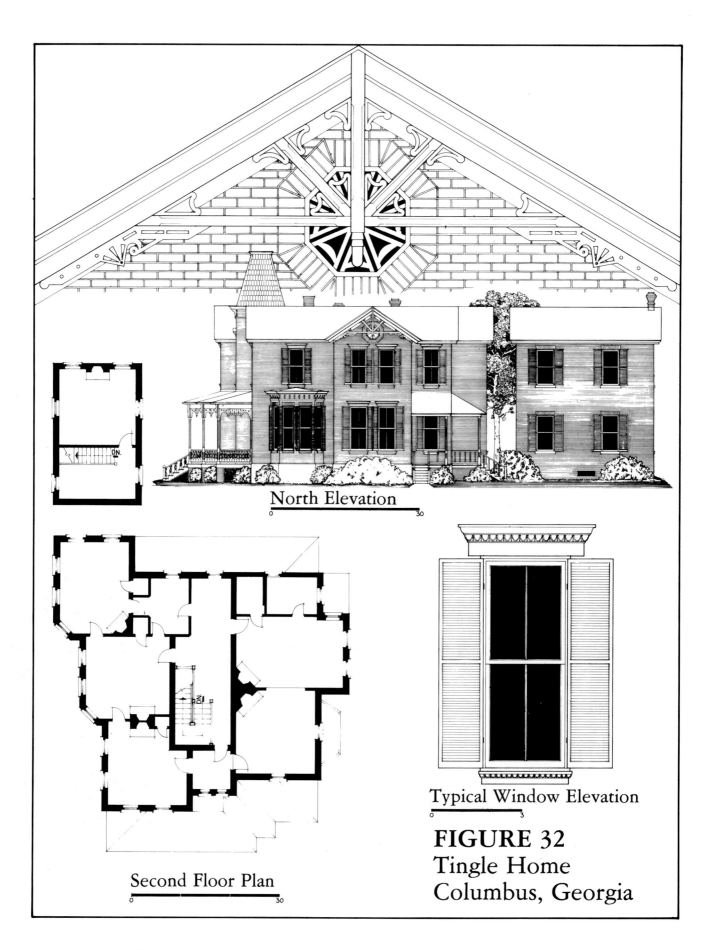

North Elevation

0   30

Typical Window Elevation

0   3

FIGURE 32
Tingle Home
Columbus, Georgia

Second Floor Plan

0   30

Tingle Home

One of the most massive Victorian houses in the Lower Chattahoochee Valley was the Tingle Home (Figures 32, 33). It was the only brick Victorian home included in the study and was truly an endangered structure. Efforts to sell the house were unsuccessful, and it was razed in June of 1976. A service station now occupies the site at 1445 Fourth Avenue in Columbus, Georgia.

Very little is known about the Tingle Home. At one time it was called the Glenn Home. In 1883 the Columbus Council purchased it for the Girls' Orphans Home to provide new and larger quarters. About 1927 Mr. and Mrs. S. C. Butler bought the house from the orphanage. Around 1949 Mrs. Butler sold the house to Dr. Jeptha Berner Tingle, a local chiropractor, who used it for his office a number of years.

The house was an example of the Italianate Victorian style. The central tower was a definitive feature, as was the bracketing under the tower, bay, and porch eaves. The windows were large and consisted of a typical two over two pane design. The window caps and sills were heavy and of a modified egg and dart motif. Under each gable was an interesting fretwork of sawn wood. Each gable also had an ornate exhaust grate of octagonal design. There was rather elaborate cutwork for porch gingerbread and balusters. A second building existed behind the main house. Assumption is that it served as servants' quarters.

Nothing is known about the interior detail of the house. It exhibited the randomness of arrangement characteristic of the style. Rooms were large with numerous windows. All main rooms had a fireplace, certainly coal burning. Ceilings would have been high, possibly as much as 12–14 feet. In all likelihood there would have been wainscoting, and possibly some exposed beams, finished in natural oak or pine. Aging of the shellac would have given a mellow, heavy look to the rooms. Mantels would have been large, even massive in the parlors, with candle brackets and beveled mirrors. It is sad when such a structure must succumb to "progress." In its day the Tingle Home would have epitomized status.

FIGURE 33
Tingle Home

East Elevation

0   30

First Floor Plan

0   30

Tingle Home.
Front view.

FIGURE 34
Bullard-Hart Home
Columbus, Georgia

Bullard-Hart Home

One of the most elegant structures in the Lower Chattahoochee Valley is the Bullard-Hart Home in Columbus, Georgia (Figures 34–37). The house sits in one of the city's former fashionable residential areas. It is an imposing structure of wood in the Second Empire Victorian style. Although the style was popular during the mid nineteenth century in Europe, its influence persisted into the late nineteenth century in America. The Bullard-Hart Home was built during the period 1887–1890. We are especially fortunate in having detailed historical information on the house.

The structure was designed by L. E. Thornton and Company of New York City. It is said that the builders, Jackson and Tinsley, went bankrupt during its construction as a result of extravagancy of detail. It was finished by the architect and decorated by the Le Rolle Company of New York City. The house was built for Dr. William Lewis Bullard and his family—his wife, the former Mary Blackmar, and daughters Elmira, Louise, and Dana. Dr. Bullard was born in Tenneville, Georgia, on February 29, 1852, the son of Elmira and Lewis Bullard. He attended Emory University and Johns Hopkins. He further pursued his medical studies in London and Vienna and eventually became a prominent eye, ear, nose, and throat specialist in Columbus.

Mrs. Bullard's family was prominent in Columbus society. The Blackmars had been in Columbus since 1835 and contributed greatly to the cultural and economic growth of the city.

The Bullards raised three daughters in the house, two of whom were married there. Elmira (Mrs. William Thomas Hart) married and lived in the house until recently. Under her supervision many prominent American citizens were graciously entertained. Franklin D. Roosevelt was a frequent visitor, even announcing his decision to run for governor of New York from the parlor on a nationwide broadcast. Other prominent guests were General George Patton, General George C. Marshall, and Supreme Court Justice Thomas Murphy.

The Bullard-Hart Home is constructed of wood. Even a cursory glance tells one that a

Bullard-Hart Home.
Front view.

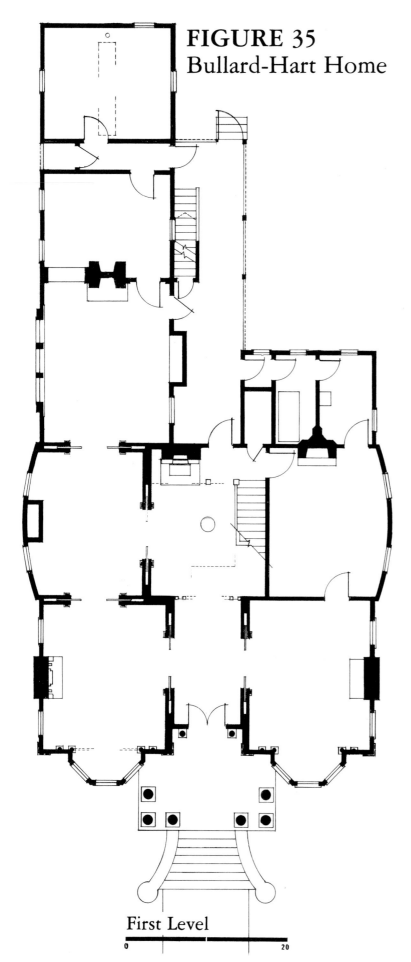

FIGURE 35
Bullard-Hart Home

First Level

0   20

great deal of time and money went into the design and construction of the house. Eclecticism is very evident. The high mansard roof and dormer windows are defining features of the Second Empire style. Bay windows are characteristic of the Queen Anne style, as are the classically detailed chimneys. The heavy eave brackets are reminiscent of the Italianate style and the delicate wrought-iron cresting is Eastlake. Windows are oversized and have large panes. The entrance is heavy and ornate. Flanked by fluted Corinthian columns on scroll bases, the whole doorway is a study in itself. There are a fanlight of stained glass, carved oak doors, heavy brass escutcheon and, not to be underemphasized, beautiful etched door panels with the Bullard initial. The chimneys are also ornate and display true artistry and craftsmanship.

The interior is no less imposing. The walls of the hallway are covered in a fabric of embossed silver, gold, and copper known as Lincrustia Walton. The ceiling is of pressed leather. The outer and inner halls incorporate a lincrustia design employing embossed paper, pressed leather, tin, and wood reliefs. The wainscoting of the inner hall is entirely of pressed leather. The hall floor is oak and pecan parquetry laid by a master craftsman from Massachusetts.

In the rear hall a spectacular staircase rises three floors, lavishly decorated with newel posts, arches, and carved balusters. A brass chandelier is suspended some thirty feet to illuminate three floors. The Bullard-Hart Home is reputed to have been the first residence in Columbus to have electricity. Mrs. Bullard, not having complete confidence in electricity, had the gas chandeliers throughout wired in such a way that gas and electricity could be used at the same time.

FIGURE 36
Bullard-Hart Home

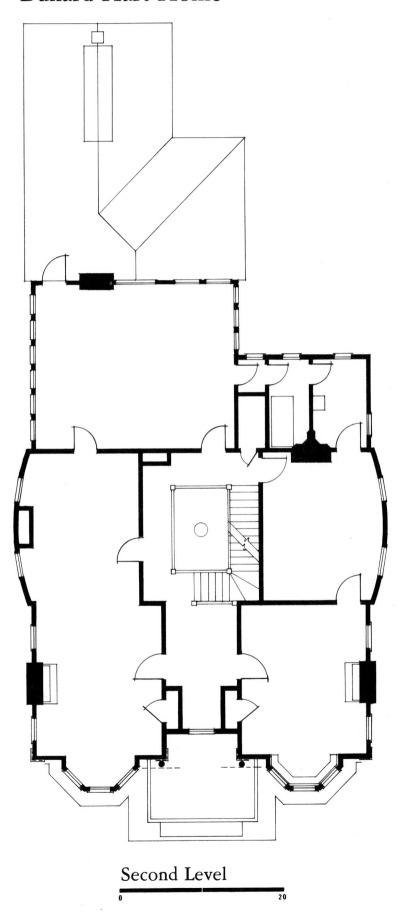

Second Level

0   20

Bullard-Hart Home.
Front entrance. Note the etched,
initialed panes and the stained-glass fanlight.

The house has been altered very little since it was built. Originally there was a ballroom on the third floor that has since been converted into bedrooms. The rear upstairs porch was enclosed with oak wainscoting and stained-glass windows to form a billiards room. The ceiling sports a beautifully ornate, exposed beam grid. The house has been fortunate in receiving better than average care but stands in need of protection. Until recently it was the home of the curator of the Columbus Museum of Arts and Crafts and his wife. The house has been placed on the National Register of Historic Places and has been purchased by Dr. and Mrs. Lloyd Sampson, who plan to restore it.

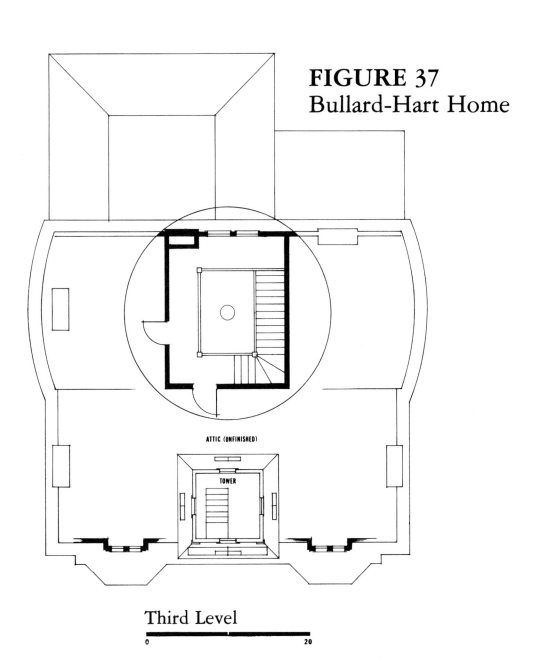

FIGURE 37
Bullard-Hart Home

ATTIC (UNFINISHED)

TOWER

Third Level

0   20

Bullard-Hart Home.
Detail of chimney and mansard roof.

Bullard-Hart Home.
Staircase detail.

Bullard-Hart Home.
Example of pressed leather on walls.

Bullard-Hart Home.
Example of pressed leather on walls.

Key Gazebo-Greenhouse.
Exterior view.

Key Gazebo-Greenhouse

The Key Gazebo-Greenhouse (Figure 38) reflects Victorian style in adjunct buildings. It is said that slaves from the Virginia plantation of Jesse Bibb Key built the octagon-shaped gazebo in 1842. Although there is local feeling that the structure is Jeffersonian in style, little evidence supports that thesis. The octagon as a popular building mode was not widespread until after the Civil War. It is inferred that it would be no less so for outbuildings than for houses. The only assumed Jeffersonian feature might be the use of fluted columns, which Jefferson did not prefer in the first place. In all likelihood the gazebo is a late Victorian structure of the Georgian or Neoclassical revivals. The heavy brackets under the eaves that serve as pseudocapitals, the smaller cyma-curved brackets, and the scalloped motif on the face of the eaves are late Victorian influence, possibly 1880–1890.

The gazebo-greenhouse is on the grounds of the old Key home, once known as Bedford Hall, in Cuthbert, Randolph County, Georgia. Jesse Bibb Key came from Bedford County, Virginia, to Cuthbert between 1835 and 1838. Mr. Key established a mercantile business and was a successful merchant for thirty years. Until recently, the property remained in the hands of direct descendants, Mrs. W. P. Smith and Miss Sarah H. Crook. The property has been purchased by Mr. Tommy Barr, who plans to restore the house and gazebo.

FIGURE 38
Key Gazebo-Greenhouse
Cuthbert, Georgia

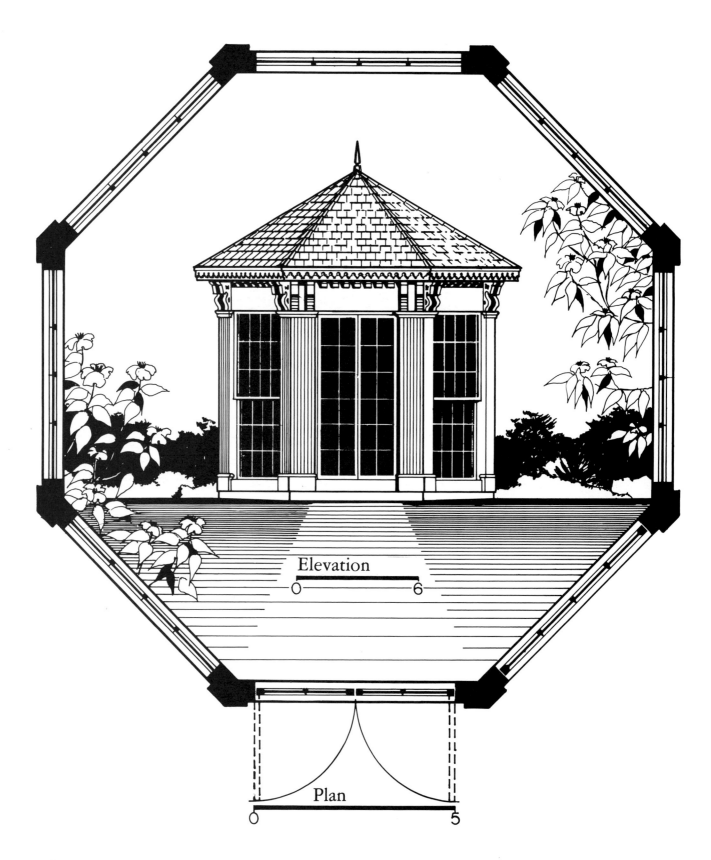

Elevation

0 — 6

Plan

0 — 5

Key Gazebo-Greenhouse.
Detail of eave.

Key Gazebo-Greenhouse.
Interior view.

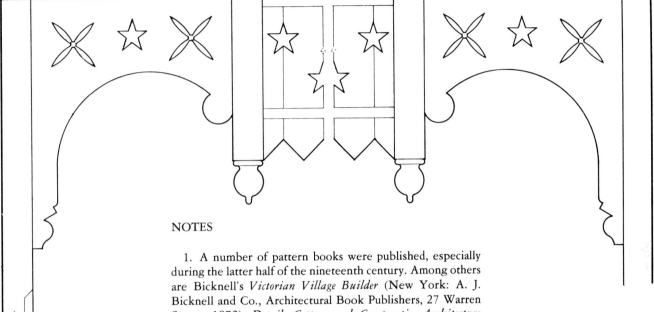

NOTES

1. A number of pattern books were published, especially during the latter half of the nineteenth century. Among others are Bicknell's *Victorian Village Builder* (New York: A. J. Bicknell and Co., Architectural Book Publishers, 27 Warren Street, 1872); *Detail, Cottage and Constructive Architecture* (New York: A. J. Bicknell and Co., Architectural Book Publishers, 27 Warren Street, 1873); *Modern Architectural Designs and Details* (New York, William T. Comstock, Architectural Publisher, 194 Broadway, 1881); and *Palliser's New Cottage Homes and Details* (New York: Palliser, Palliser, and Co., 1887).

2. Downing wrote a number of books that influenced the taste of mid nineteenth-century America. Among the more important were: *Cottage Residences,* first published in 1842 and going through twelve editions by 1888; and *The Architecture of Country Houses,* first published in 1850. By the end of the Civil War it had gone through nine printings.

3. I have drawn freely from Clay Lancaster's analysis of Victorian styles as presented in his introduction to *Victorian Houses: A Treasury of Lesser-Known Examples,* Edmund V. Gillon, Jr., and Clay Lancaster (New York: Dover Publications, 1973).

CHAPTER FIVE

Architectural Potpourri-I

THE BUILDINGS included in this chapter cover a range of architectural styles and a wide historical span. They are grouped here because each shares the common trait of serving a particular public use. The structures are all non-domestic, that is, they are not or were not used as domiciles. Included are a bank, church, school, mill, doctor's office, stores, depot, and jails.

Bank of Seale

Dating from about 1909, the Bank of Seale (Figure 39) is built in a style reminiscent of that of Louis Henry Sullivan (termed, by Whiffen, "Sullivanesque"), which was popular in the late nineteenth and early twentieth centuries. This style is characterized by simple forms, flat roofs, and boldly projecting cornices. The style was introduced by Sullivan in 1890 and was widely used for commercial buildings throughout the United States.

The first bank in Seale was not housed in this structure but was in a corner of the Anderson-Benton Cotton Warehouse. Early stockholders of the Bank of Seale included H. T. Benton, W. T. Anderson, Ed Anderson, W. E. Starke (or Stark), the Charles Hill Tigner Estate, Erin de Lacy Boykin, and F. M. deGraffenried. The name of the bank was changed to The First National Bank of Seale in 1914.

The bank failed in the late 1920s. Internal mismanagement and the Depression were contributing factors. Being the largest financial institution in Russell County, its failure was seen as the beginning of Seale's decline as the major commercial center of the county. The dominance of nearby Columbus, Georgia, has had its effect upon Seale's ability to regain its former status.

The structure is built entirely of brick using common bond. The walls are 12 inches thick and structurally good, although the finish is poor. The plan is rectangular with the former vault the only interior addition. The interior walls are stuccoed and the ceiling is pressed metal, a common material of the times. While not glamorous, the structure is indicative of commercial buildings erected in towns across America around the turn of the century. The building is presently unoccupied.

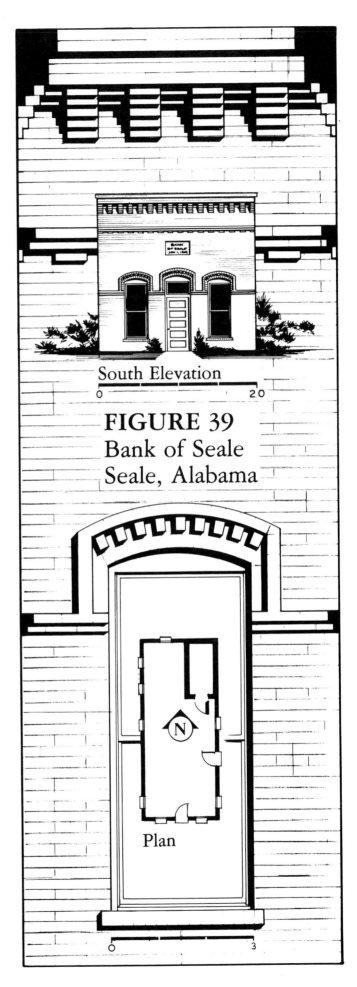

South Elevation

0   20

FIGURE 39
Bank of Seale
Seale, Alabama

Plan

0   3

Bank of Seale.
Exterior view.

Bank of Seale.
Detail of front facade.
Note the fancy brickwork.

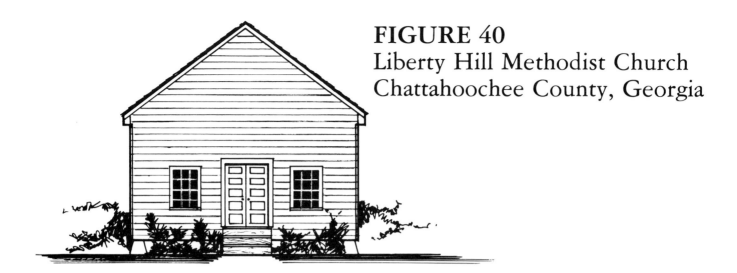

FIGURE 40
Liberty Hill Methodist Church
Chattahoochee County, Georgia

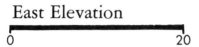

East Elevation

0   20

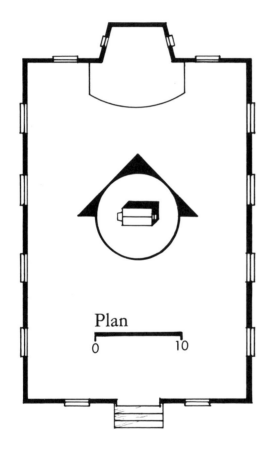

Plan

0   10

Liberty Hill Methodist Church

Typical of the small rural churches found scattered throughout the early settled areas of the South is the Liberty Hill Methodist Church (Figure 40). A plain structure possessing no architectural frivolity, it perhaps is closer in style to a frontier building than a Greek Revival structure. The present church is not the first Liberty Hill Methodist Church. A log church and its cemetery were established early in the first half of the nineteenth century. The oldest grave in the cemetery dates back to 1854.

David Gaskins McGlaun gave the land for the church and cemetery. In 1828 this land was in Lee County, Georgia. Later, as county lines were realigned, it became a part of Muscogee and then Marion County, and in 1854 it became part of Chattahoochee County. The early minutes of the church have been lost. Minutes from March 6, 1869, however, contain a reference to the formation of a committee to repair the church building. It seems safe to assume that this reference is to the present structure. In the 1869 revision of the church roster Starling Dillard was listed as having joined in 1862. It is conceivable that the church house could date that early.

The plan is rectangular with a single entrance

in the west gable end. It is difficult to state for sure, but there is a possibility that the front windows were originally doors and that the entrance was a window as in the churches at Uchee. A post–Civil War date seems more likely, however, as the characteristic antebellum feature of separate entrance and seating area for the slaves is absent. Another significant change in the church's plan is that the building has a small apse and podium in the rear. The interior walls and ceilings are of beaded tongue and groove lumber, yet another index to a postbellum origin.

The church structure has undergone few changes since its origin. A covered stoop and cement steps were added in November of 1949. In 1969 some of the sills were repaired.

Liberty Hill Methodist Church disbanded in December 1969, when membership had dwindled to three. It is not possible to list all the families that have figured prominently in the church's history. From the 1869 roster a few of the early members were: David G. McGlaun, Mrs. Vesta Brewer, William Lane, Jonathan T. Roberson, Starling M. Dillard, James Duncan, and Cornelius Barbaree. The picturesque little white church stands empty now, but nestled in its grove of pines and moss-draped oaks, it is truly a quiet place where one can worship God in tranquility.

Liberty Hill Methodist Church.
Exterior view. The small porch is an addition.

A. D. McLain Building

Reminiscent of other rural Southern commercial buildings of the early twentieth century, the A. D. McLain Building stands neglected in Salem, Alabama (Figure 41). Facts about the building and its owner are sparse. Dr. McLain maintained his office in the building as well as a drugstore. At one time the post office was also there; the building is known to most people as the old post office. Dr. McLain came to Salem long before 1900. Some time after settling, he married Miss Willie Taylor. Exactly when his office and drugstore were built is not known; a reasonable guess is the first decade of the twentieth century. Until 1915 he had a partner, a druggist, by the name of Conway Harris. Locals well remember the old soda fountain in the store. After Mrs. McLain's death in April 1959, the building was sold to the Dudley Lumber Company.

The building is rather spartan; it is constructed of heart pine and has had numerous alterations through the years. Which of the two rear rooms was clinic and which was office simply cannot be ascertained. The post office was an addition to the rear room on the southwest. There was a single chimney with three flues; each room had its own fireplace. The building is used for storage today and is in fair condition.

A. D. McLain Building.
Front view.

FIGURE 41
A. D. McLain Building
Salem, Alabama

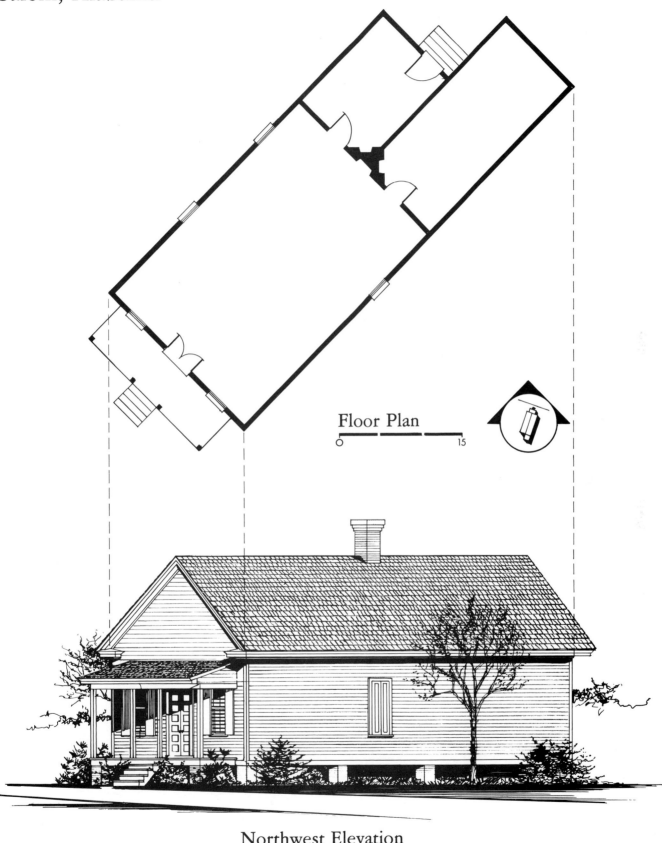

Floor Plan
0   15

Northwest Elevation
0   25

Barbour County High School

Under the administration of Governor B. B. Comer, legislation was passed enabling each Alabama county to have a high school partially supported by state funds. The Barbour County Board of Education offered the school to Clayton, Louisville, and Clio. Clio was able to secure the funds necessary to build the structure (Figure 42); Eufaula was not in the running because it already had a high school. The Barbour County High School was constructed in 1908–1909 by W. G. Lunsford, a local contractor, and was dedicated in 1910 with appropriate ceremonies and dignitaries. The first principal was Dan McLean, a Clio native; the first

Barbour County High School.
North elevation.
The original portico is gone as is the cupola.

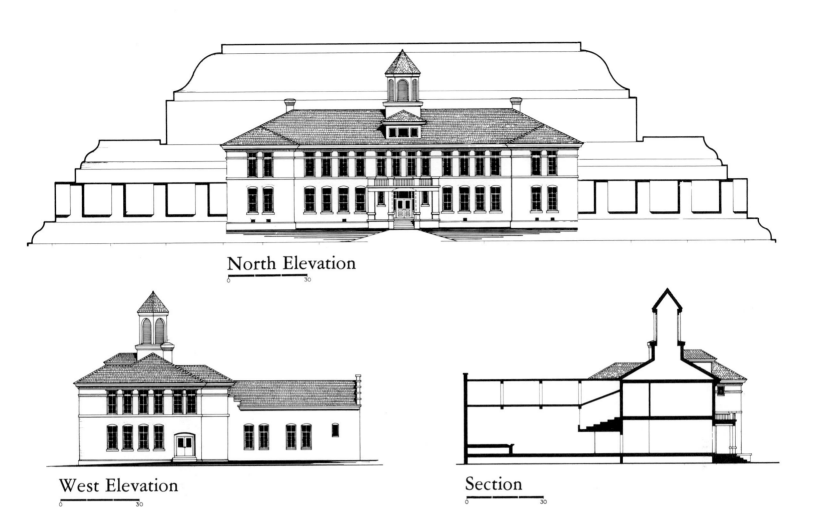

North Elevation

West Elevation

Section

First and Second Floor Plans

2nd addition

1st addition

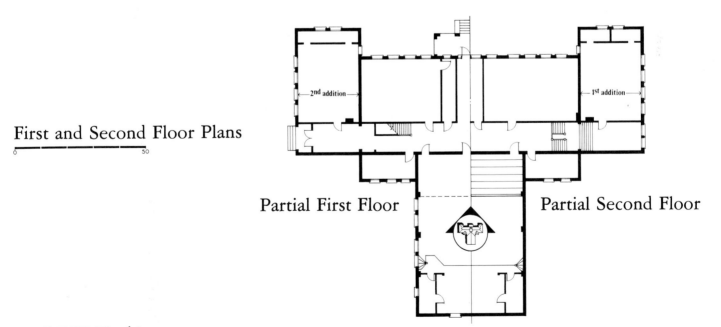

Partial First Floor

Partial Second Floor

FIGURE 42
Barbour County High School
Clio, Alabama

Barbour County High School.
View of the stage in the auditorium.

teachers were Ernest W. Norton, Lewe Dorman, and Miss Ethel Stephenson. A boarding house for county students was built across the street from the school. Its most well-known graduate is George C. Wallace, Governor of Alabama.

The school cannot be easily categorized architecturally. A number of motifs and features of various styles are incorporated. Its symmetry would indicate Neoclassical or possibly Georgian Revival. The portico is gone. Additions were made in 1937–1938 and in 1940. It was at these times that the wings were added; Henderson, Black, and Greene of Troy, Alabama, were the contractors.

The school graduated classes until recently

with the exception of 1934 when Alabama public schools were forced to close for lack of funds. The school is not in use at present. The Board of Education has deeded the structure to the George C. Wallace Heritage Association, which is currently seeking funds to restore the school as a civic center and museum for Wallace memorabilia. The State of Alabama has contributed $25,000; an additional gift of $975 from Faulkner State Junior College has strengthened the program.

Barbour County High School.
View of auditorium and balcony.

FIGURE 43
Vicksburg and Brunswick Depot
Eufaula, Alabama

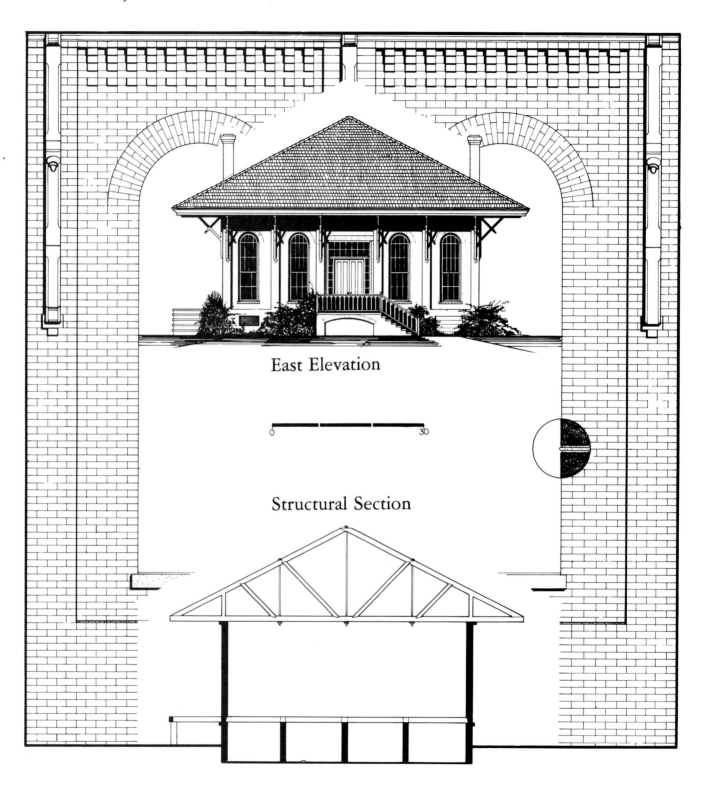

East Elevation

0   30

Structural Section

Vicksburg and Brunswick Depot

This interesting structure, the Vicksburg and Brunswick Depot, is representative of the substantial type of structure built during the heyday of the American railway industry (Figures 43, 44). The railroads moved America's manufactured and raw materials. Great pride was taken by towns in their depots, and many were elaborate edifices, symbols of the town's prosperity. The Vicksburg and Brunswick depot was originally constructed in 1872 for the V. and B. Railroad Company as a combination passenger and freight terminal. The V. and B. Railroad Company was organized under an act of the Alabama Legislature on January 23, 1867, for the purpose of building a railroad from Eufaula to Meridian, Mississippi, via Troy, Greenville, and Camden, Alabama. John Hardy, John Gill Shorter, and D. M. Seals were prominent Barbour County citizens involved in the organization.

The railroad never got past Clayton, Ala-

Vicksburg and Brunswick Depot. Exterior view.

bama, on the originally projected route; the twenty-one miles were completed in 1871. In 1872 the Southwest Railroad Company leased the line, but by 1879 the line was up for sale at foreclosure proceedings. It had endorsed $300,000 worth of Barbour County bonds and could not pay the interest. Liability for payment eventually evolved on Southwestern's creditor, the Central Railroad and Banking Company of Georgia, which purchased the railroad for $80,000 to protect its credit.

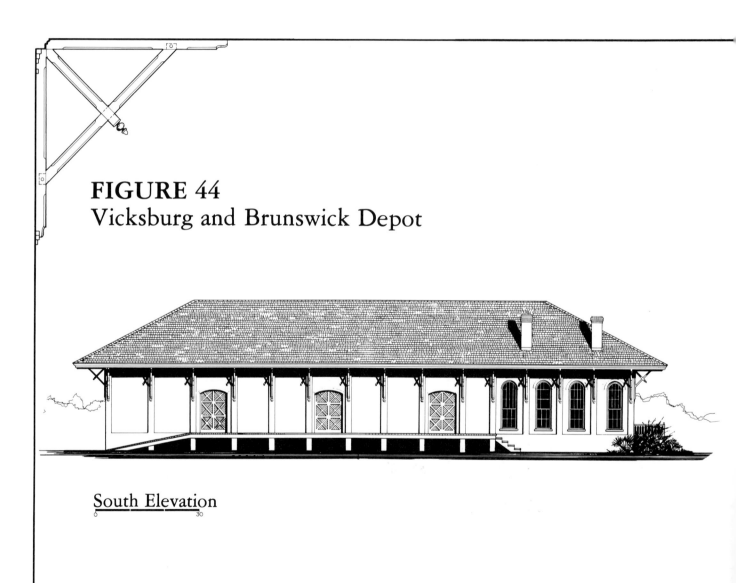

FIGURE 44
Vicksburg and Brunswick Depot

South Elevation

In 1883 the railroad was reorganized as the Eufaula and Clayton Railroad. W. G. Raoul was elected president, Ed McIntyre secretary, and as directors, J. E. Jones, T. B. Gresham, G. L. Comer, and George H. Dent. By 1888 the railroad had been extended to Ozark, a distance of forty miles. For a time the building in Eufaula was known as the Eufaula and Ozark Depot. In 1891 a new depot was finally built in a different location as a result of public demand and the poor condition of the old structure. Shortly

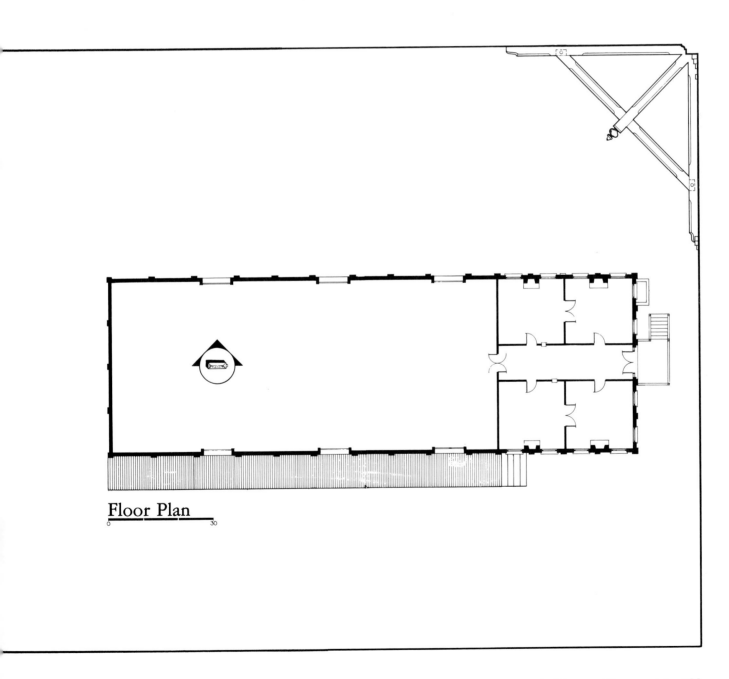

Floor Plan

Vicksburg and Brunswick Depot.
View of entrance. Note the arched windows.

after the depot was constructed, the railroad declined in importance, so the building was seldom used for the railroad. It was leased for various purposes until 1948, when it was sold to the Eufaula Hardware Company for a warehouse.

The depot is an imposing structure of brick with walls 12 inches thick. The roof trusses are supported by brick pilasters built up the exterior walls. Each pilaster has a wooden bracket as decoration and as additional support for the broad overhang of the roof that forms a shelter for the docks. Each truss is made from three 2 x 12 inch beams that are spliced and bolted together.

The doors and windows are unusually large. The windows are interesting in that they are arched on the exterior but finished square on the interior and shuttered. The four front rooms served as offices and as a passenger waiting area. The bulk of the space was used for storage. The building is in fair shape and could be an interesting functional restoration project. Similar depots have been converted to restaurants, boutiques, flea market facilities, and the like.

Vicksburg and Brunswick Depot.
View down side along the loading platform.
Note the brackets, the tremendous trusses they partially support,
and the old advertisements painted on the walls.

Vicksburg and Brunswick Depot.
Detail of storage area door
and advertisements painted on walls.

Meadows Mill

In Lee County, Alabama, Meadows Mill is representative of the type of gristmill one might have encountered a century ago (Figure 45). Only the mill remains of what was once a thriving industrial complex; the cotton gin, sawmill, and store are gone. The mill is known to have existed since the 1870s; it is probably antebellum. The Meadows were not the original owners. David and Lucy Fuller transferred a quarter interest (1/4) in the mills and ten acres of associated land to Daniel P. Meadows on January 27, 1873. The remaining three-quarters (3/4) interest appears to have been held by the McKinnon family (variously spelled, including McKennon and McKenon).

Meadows Mill.
Front view.
The shed across the front is an addition.

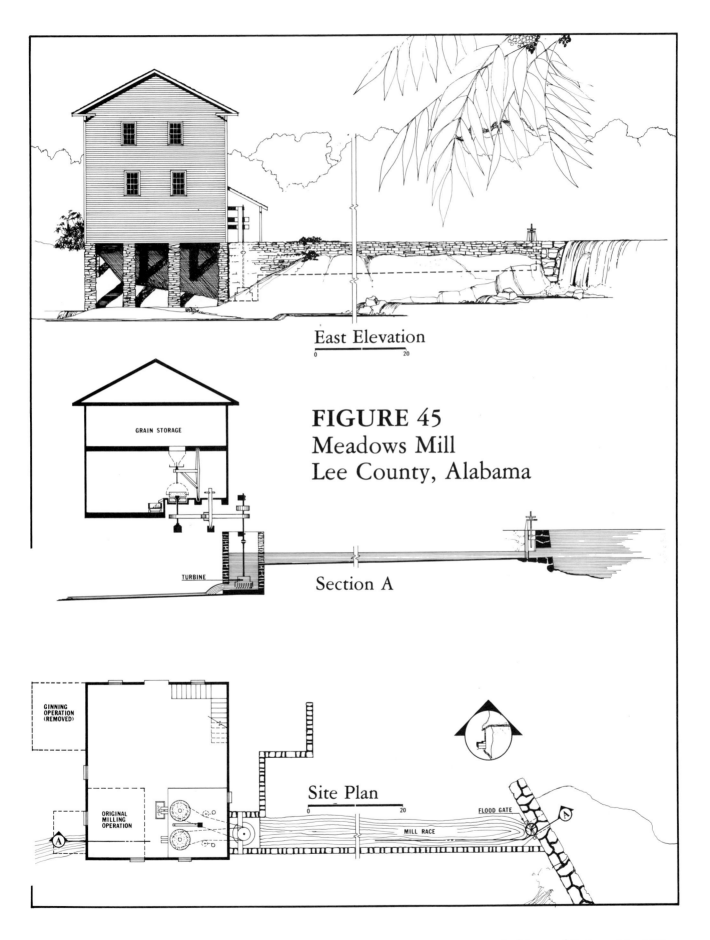

East Elevation

0   20

FIGURE 45
Meadows Mill
Lee County, Alabama

GRAIN STORAGE

TURBINE

Section A

GINNING
OPERATION
(REMOVED)

ORIGINAL
MILLING
OPERATION

Site Plan

0   20

FLOOD GATE

MILL RACE

Most deeds refer to the property as the McKinnon Mill.

In 1909 George W. McKinnon gave his interest in the mill to his wife, Mary E. McKinnon, and his three children—Fletcher, John, and Nellie. By 1911 Mrs. McKinnon and Nellie (Mrs. John C. Wade) had acquired the 3/4 interest. Later that year D. P. Meadows bought the remaining 3/4 interest in the mill from the McKinnon family for $1600. The mill remained in the Meadows estate until acquired by its present owner, G. L. Story, in 1957. The mill was operable until 1971.

The 1880 Census of Manufacturing of the United States contains the following informa-

Meadows Mill.
Southern exposure.
The original milling equipment was in the lower right corner of this view.

Meadows Mill.
Detail of the supports.
Note the mortise and tenon construction.

Meadows Mill.
The mill dam.

Meadows Mill.
Detail of the water housing beneath the mill.

tion on the mill: The mill belonged to George McKevon (McKinnon); there was a capital investment of $3500; two hands were employed most of the year; mill operated on a 12-hour day from November to May; skilled laborers earned $1/day, unskilled earned $.50/day; two runs of stones with an estimated daily capacity of 60 bushels; produced 1200 barrels of flour, 270,000 pounds of cornmeal, and 69,200 pounds of feed. The total value for all products was $11,363. Comparison of data from mills of similar size throughout the South suggests that Meadows Mill was typical.

Meadows Mill was turbine-powered; one of the turbines is still in place. The mill head, the height of the drop of water, is approximately twelve feet and was used to power two turbines. The building has two stories, the upper used for storage and machinery. On the lower floor the milling operation took place. The mill's frame is entirely built of heart pine lumber, which is pegged together. Siding is clapboard nailed with square-headed nails. The outside foundations, the millrace, and the dam are of stone. The original roof was wooden shingles.

The interior is spacious and unfinished. The most significant feature is the hurst, or milling floor. This elevated floor has the millstones, stone crane, disengager for the pulleys, and the like. Meal would fall from the hurst through a chute into a bin where it was scooped up and sacked. The mill is in fair condition and could be restored with a minimum of expense. Similar restorations have made popular working museums or craft shops.

Meadows Mill.
The stone crane with one of the stones.

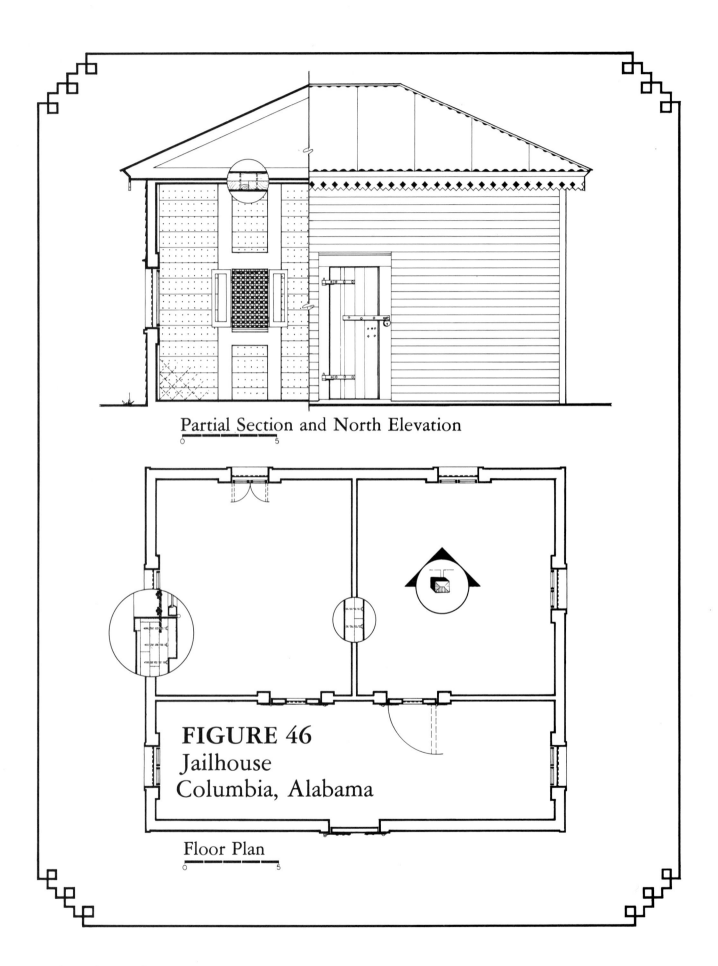

Partial Section and North Elevation

0   5

FIGURE 46
Jailhouse
Columbia, Alabama

Floor Plan

0   5

Columbia Jailhouse

Little attention is usually accorded less popular public buildings, and jails are especially neglected. The jailhouse at Columbia, Houston County, Alabama, is an interesting structure with some architectural merit (Figure 46). The little building dates from the latter part of the nineteenth century. In 1885 Captain John T. Davis conveyed a tract of land in downtown Columbia to the "Mayor and the Council of Columbia and their successors forever." This tract of land contained the jail, city hall, and other buildings. Exactly when the jail was constructed is not known, possibly as early as the 1870s.

Whether the original plan included four cells or two is a question of debate among locals. It once contained three rooms, a large room across the front measuring approximately 6 x 21 feet and two adjoining cells 10 x 10 feet. Alterations have been made, converting the jail into one large room. Windows were installed behind the bars and new flooring was put down. The entire structure is of wood with walls 8 to 10 inches thick. An interesting feature is that the walls are covered with closely spaced iron spikes to deter escape attempts by sawing through the walls. There are no chimneys or fireplaces, so the building was undoubtedly very cold in winter. The structure is significant as an example of public architecture; common service buildings seldom survive long. The jail has served as a library and now is a museum.

Columbia Jailhouse.
Exterior. Note the Victorian gingerbread.

Columbia Jailhouse.
Detail of the window, exterior.

Columbia Jailhouse.
Door. Note the thickness of the walls.

Quitman County Jail

Another public building that has been spared demolition is the Quitman County Jail (Figure 47). The jail was designed by the Commissioners of Quitman County, Georgia, in 1890–1891. The committee included J. E. Harris, Dr. F. M. Bledsoe, J. P. Kimble, and W. A. Cumbie. J. E. Harris was the representative to the legislature from the county. Built in 1891, the structure was originally surrounded by a tall wooden wall. There was a windmill to provide water.

The jail is substantially constructed, built entirely of brick, using a common bond. The walls are 12 inches thick. The second floor is concrete over a first floor ceiling of corrugated metal bearing on I beams. The result has the effect of a multivaulted ceiling. The interior walls are plastered and painted white. The cell windows are built using a grid of four flat horizontal bars and nine vertical round ones. Metal thresholds at the entrance to cells read "Quitman County, 1891."

The building has been given by the Commissioners to the Georgetown Garden Club for restoration. It is indeed fortunate that Quitman County's oldest structure will be preserved for future generations.

Quitman County Jail.
East elevation.

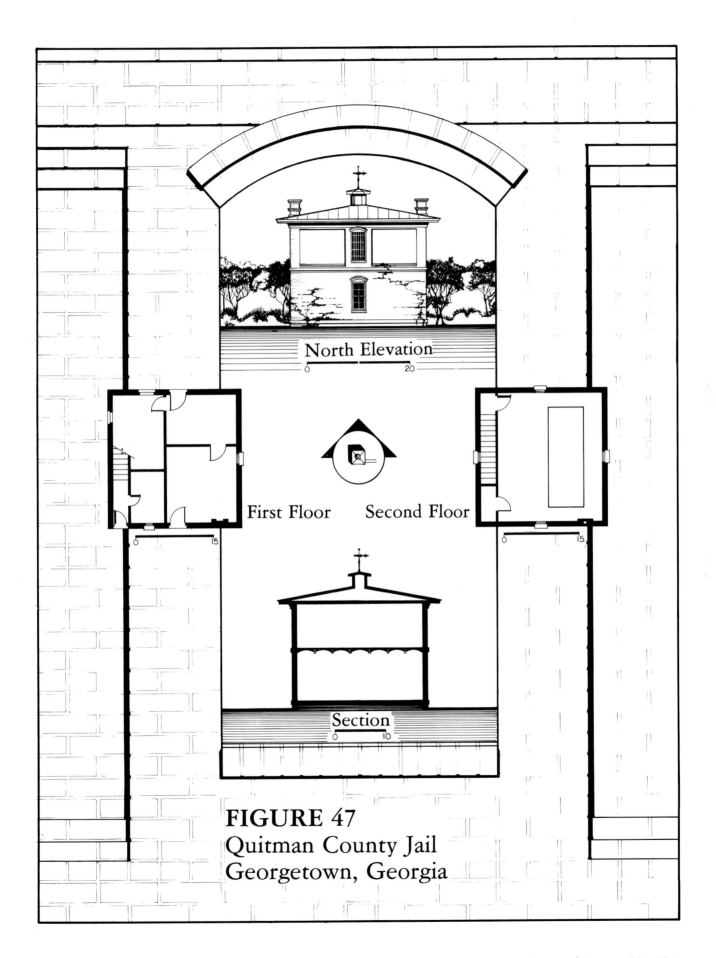

North Elevation

0   20

First Floor   Second Floor

0   15   0   15

Section

0   10

FIGURE 47
Quitman County Jail
Georgetown, Georgia

Wagnon-Mitchell-Samford Store

A type of general commercial building encountered in small towns across the South at the turn of the century is represented by the Wagnon-Mitchell-Samford Store (Figure 48), in Opelika, Lee County, Alabama. The structure dates from the early 1880s; the first reference to a business on the lot was in 1884. The original owner and proprietor was J. E. Wagnon. The property passed through the hands of a number of individuals after 1894; among the owners were J. W. Burke (1894–1913), Charles J. Burke (1913–1915), E. A. Burke (1915–1945), G. A. Mitchell (1945–1958). Mrs. Evlyn B. Samford acquired the property in 1958 and is still owner. J. P. Ennis operated a grocery store in the building from the 1950s to the early 1970s. At present the building is unoccupied.

Wagnon-Mitchell-Samford Store.
Exterior view.
Note the brick coping. The awning is not original.

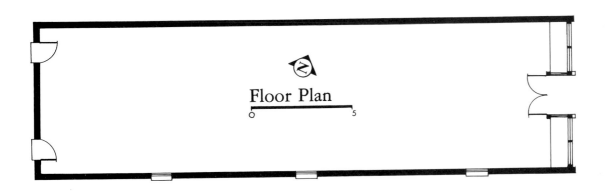

Floor Plan

FIGURE 48
Wagnon-Mitchell-Samford Store
Opelika, Alabama

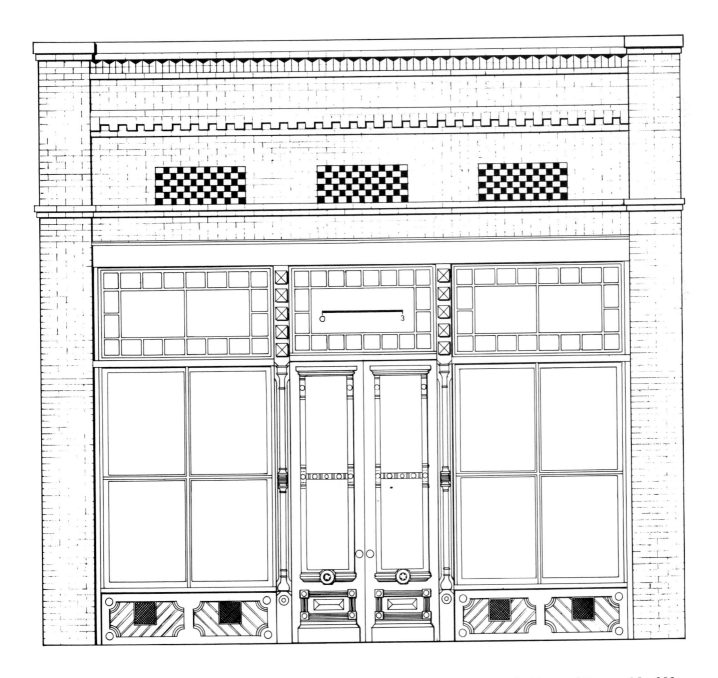

Wagnon-Mitchell-Samford Store.
Front facade. Note the design in the brickwork.

The store is a fine example of the Eastlake and Queen Anne Victorian influence in commercial architecture. The Queen Anne influence is clearly seen in the small, multicolored glass panes around the upper portions of the display windows. The Eastlake influence is evident in the door treatments and in the use of wooden rosettes in numerous places. In addition there is interesting design work in the brick facade above the windows. The sides have brick coping in a step design. Although in disrepair, the building is of significance because its attractive facade has not been substantially altered. A drive through any railroad town of the rural South will yield numerous similar examples, though commonly their attractiveness has been lessened by "modernization."

Wagnon-Mitchell-Samford Store.
Detail of the woodwork.
Note the Eastlake style rosettes.

CHAPTER SIX

Architectural Potpourri-II

THE REMAINING STRUCTURES included in this chapter are singly representative of a certain style or do not fit neatly into any recognized style; they have been grouped here for expediency. Within this assortment of structures are a courthouse, covered bridge, miscellaneous plantation outbuildings, some houses, a barn, and a variety of grave shelters. Each in its own way has merit and deserves public attention because of its significance as a part of our cultural heritage. It is hoped that protection of such structures will be assured through public appreciation.

Gold Hill Commissary

Many rural communities in the Lower Chattahoochee Valley had commissaries. The structure at Gold Hill, Lee County, Alabama, is one of the larger and better preserved in the area (Figure 49). The building standing today is the second such store on the site. George Cherry first built a commissary there around 1880. A second structure, the present building, was built on the site around 1905–1906 by J. E. Ellington, Mr. Cherry's son-in-law. Ellington operated the store until 1927 when it was acquired for debts by W. C. Bradley and Company of Columbus, Georgia. Mr. Bradley employed Ellington to run the store and a large farm until 1937, when the store ceased operation. From 1937 to 1940 the building was owned by Hugh Chandler and Judge J. L. Tyner of Opelika. Around 1950, Charlie Rush bought

Gold Hill Commissary.
South elevation.

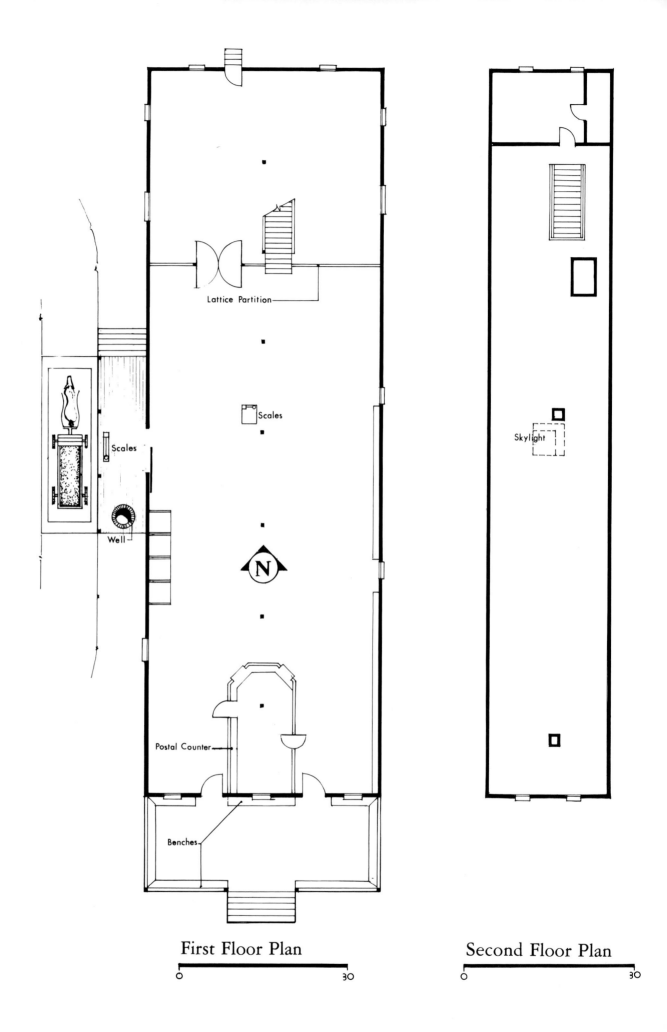

First Floor Plan

0   30

Second Floor Plan

0   30

FIGURE 49
Gold Hill Commissary
Lee County, Alabama

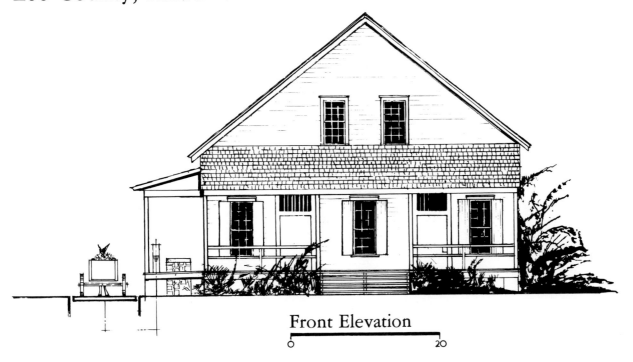

Front Elevation

0   20

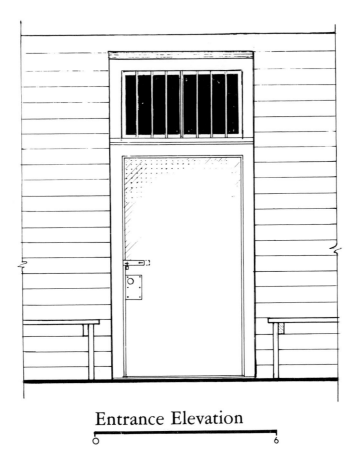

Entrance Elevation

0   6

Gold Hill Commissary.
Detail of door. Note the many nails, supposedly used to discourage
forced entry by axing or sawing through the door.

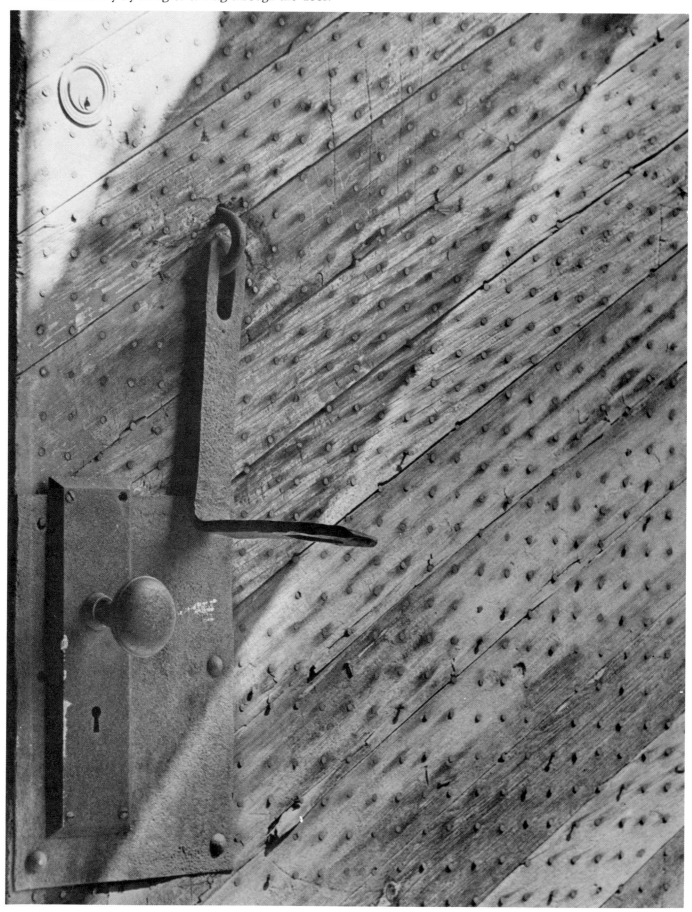

Gold Hill Commissary.
Interior view.
Note the outline on the ceiling of the former post office walls.

the property and is currently using the old store for storage.

The Gold Hill Commissary was a significant commercial enterprise serving farmers and townspeople for a radius of ten miles. In addition to the store, there was a cotton gin, a cottonseed house, a depot, and a blacksmith shop. The store was a complete service center. On the lower floor were groceries, dry goods, stoves, and agricultural hardware of every sort. The second floor was used for storage of stove pipes, coffins, some agricultural equipment, and a host of other merchandise. Virtually every needed item could be obtained in one stop. In addition the building housed a post office and a telegraph service.

The structure is off the ground and rests on stone piers. Sills are 8 x 8 inch, both hand-hewn and sawn. Some of the sills bearing the walls are variously 8 x 11 inches and 7 x 14 inches. The exterior siding is pine clapboard. The road in front of the store has been moved closer to the building, resulting in alterations to the structure. Originally a porch 16 feet deep extended across the front of the building. The shed roof was supported by four massive posts 8 inches square. Between the posts across the front, down the porch sides, and across the front of the building were benches, an important feature of such stores.

There was a second porch on the west side of the commissary where cotton, as well as other

Gold Hill Commissary.
Detail of interior lock.

heavy merchandise, was weighed. The shed roof covered a large scale for weighing wagons, as well as a smaller scale on the edge of the porch used for smaller sacks. Underneath the porch was a well.

The interior was large and open. Between the two entrances was an enclosed postal and telegraph office, complete with windows and counters. On the left as one entered were groceries, including large bins for flour and other items. On the right was the dry-goods section. About halfway back, in the center, was a set of large scales. About three-quarters of the way back was a stairway to the second floor. Slightly behind the first risers and extending across the store was a lattice partition. Large double doors to the left of the stairs gave access to the back area, which was used for the storage of stoves and farm equipment.

The second floor was a long narrow room running nearly the full length of the store. The space was used for general storage. In the rear was a small section partitioned off and used as living quarters. The area was lighted by windows, a skylight, and acetylene lamps. All lights in the store were acetylene; there was no electricity to the building while it operated as a store. Immediately behind the commissary were a blacksmith shop and an acetylene pump house; the foundations of the latter can still be seen.

Gold Hill Commissary.
Detail of interior bracing supporting the second floor. The large hooks were used for hanging merchandise on display.

Cleaveland-Godwin-Nelson-Peacock Barn

The barn (Figure 50) is an outbuilding on the Cleaveland-Godwin-Nelson-Peacock property (see pp. 62–65). Exactly when the barn was built is not known, although the large timbers in the framework and the mortise and tenon construction could indicate an early date. Sills

Cleaveland-Godwin-Nelson-Peacock Barn.
West elevation.
The shed room to the right is an addition.

FIGURE 50
Cleaveland-Godwin-Nelson-Peacock Barn
Whitesville, Georgia

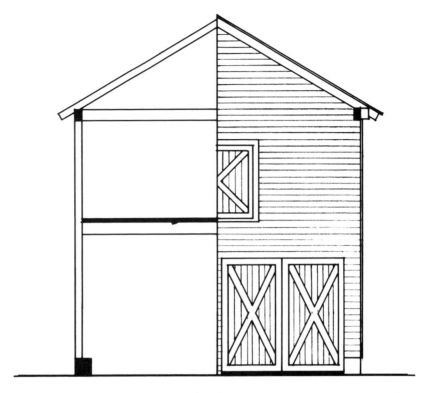

Partial Section and West Elevation

0   10

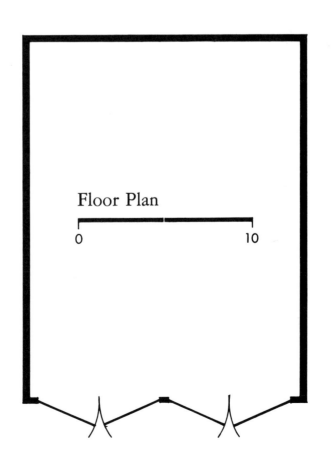

Floor Plan

0   10

are 10 x 10 inches, and other framing studs and rafters are 3 x 4 inches. Material is all heart pine and the framing is covered with 6-inch clapboard. The doors are not original.

The barn appears to have served a double function, one as storage, evidenced by the presence of a loft, and the other as a wagon or machinery shed. The absence of any stable area indicates it was not intended as an animal shelter. While the barn does not fit neatly into any of the categories established by barn scholars, it is significant in that it is an original structure that gives a very concrete idea of the types of serviceable buildings that were grouped around substantial Southern farms.

Cleaveland-Godwin-Nelson-Peacock Barn.
Detail of mortise and tenon construction.

Malone Stone House

The building reputed to be the oldest structure in Bainbridge, Georgia, is the Malone Stone House (Figure 51). History of the building can be authenticated over a span of more than 130 years. The original owner, John A. Malone, either built or had the house built before 1845. Records in the Decatur County Courthouse reveal that the property was sold at a sheriff's sale on February 25, 1845, to John Harrell. Harrell transferred the house to Mrs. Rossie Harrell Terrell in October of 1885. In 1916 Sara T. Hicks bought the property, later selling it to the Martin family, heirs of the latter now being owners. The house was used for residential as well as commercial purposes. Among the businesses conducted in the building was the law practice of Justice John Boyett.

The house was not actually constructed of stone but of brick. The walls were twelve inches thick and covered both inside and out with stucco. The exterior walls were incised to simulate stone blocks 4 feet x 1 foot in size. The roof was gabled with the surface and ends covered in wooden shingles. Locals remember a second-story porch across the front.

The interior of the house did not show much evidence of sumptuousness. The lower floor was one great room; the upper consisted of two rooms roughly equal in size. A single chimney with lower and upper stuccoed fireplaces provided the only heating. Walls were finished with stucco, and ceilings were plaster on wood lath. Evidence of circular saw marks on the ceiling lath suggests that the house was constructed post-1840. Framing was rough-sawn timber, probably pine, that varies from 2 x 6 to 2 x 12 inches.

The Malone Stone House lacked cornices and wainscoting. Windows were double-hung and had no shutters. Flooring was 1 x 4 inch tongue and groove, square-nailed. Interior trim consisted of very rough trim of varying widths and one inch thick. Historical significance lies in the fact that it was probably the oldest structure in Bainbridge until demolished in early 1977.

Malone Stone House.
Note the shingled gable and plain brackets under the eave.

FIGURE 51
Malone Stone House
Bainbridge, Georgia

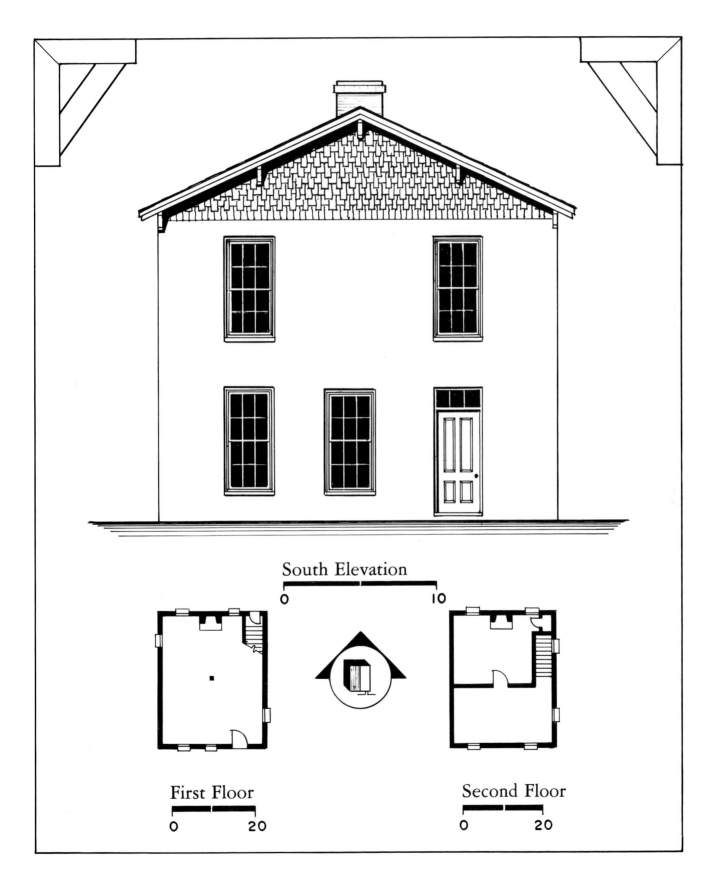

South Elevation

0   10

First Floor

0   20

Second Floor

0   20

Moye Plantation Outbuildings

The Moye Plantation, home of Mr. and Mrs. L. M. Moye, Jr., was established by David Harrell in 1836–1837 in Stewart County, Georgia. In 1853 William West, L. M. Moye's great-grandfather, purchased the plantation, his home having burned earlier that year. Mr. West deeded the house and 2,272 acres to his daughter, Annie Crooks West, in 1867. She later married James Nelson McMichael, and they lived in the plantation home until their deaths. After Mrs. McMichael died in 1915, the farm was operated by the administrators of her estate until it was purchased by her nephew, L. M. Moye, Sr., in 1929. It has since come into the

Moye Plantation.
The "Big House."

Moye Plantation.
The cook's house.

Moye Plantation.
The kitchen.

Moye Plantation.
The privy.

possession of his son. The plantation has been referred to variously as "Moye Farms," "West Hill," and the "McMichael Place." Stewart County is indeed fortunate to have such a complete assemblage of antebellum structures in one location. Among the structures built either by Harrell or West are: a privy, blacksmith's shop, five slave cabins, a kitchen, the cook's residence, a commissary, and a schoolhouse (Figures 52, 53).

Few alterations have been made in either the home or dependencies through the years. The slave cabins are empty and the privy is no longer used. The cook's house, kitchen, and blacksmith shop are a feed house, a pantry, and a farm-implement shelter respectively. The commissary is a tool room. Benches and tables

Moye Plantation.
The commissary.

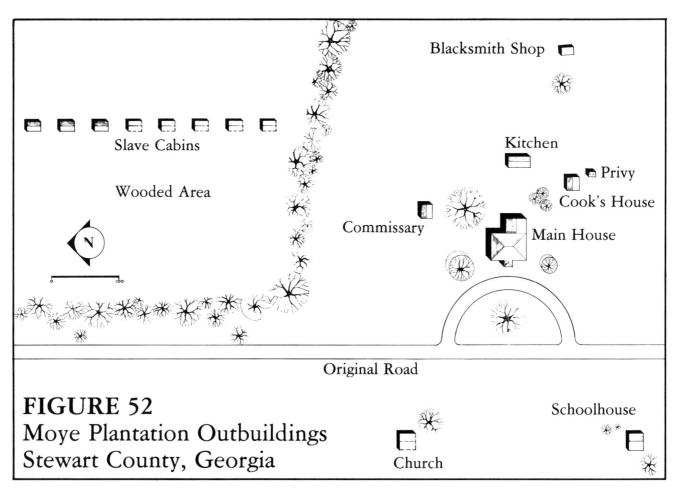

FIGURE 52
Moye Plantation Outbuildings
Stewart County, Georgia

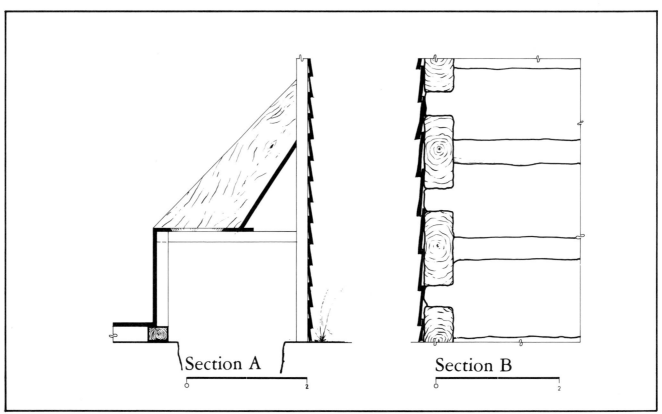

Section A

Section B

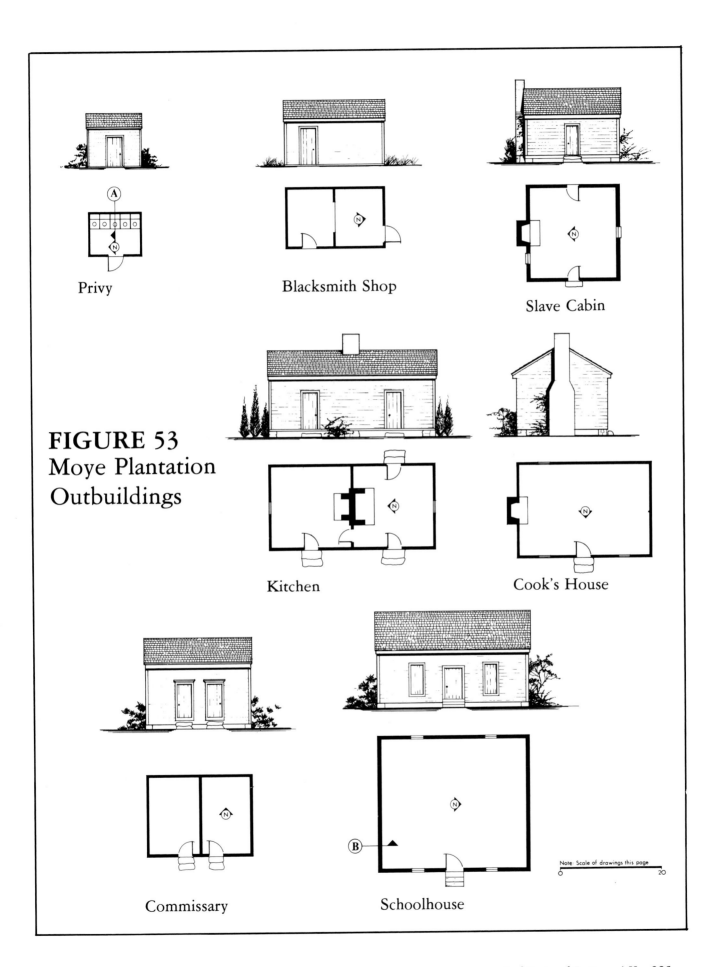

FIGURE 53
Moye Plantation
Outbuildings

Privy

Blacksmith Shop

Slave Cabin

Kitchen

Cook's House

Commissary

Schoolhouse

Note: Scale of drawings this page
0   20

have been set up in the school, and it is variously used for meetings and community suppers.

Each of the buildings exhibits some similarity of construction. All, for instance, have gabled roofs and, at one time, wooden shingles. Siding is clapboard, even over the logs in the slave cabins and the school. There was once a log church, but it has since been razed. Large sills, mortise and tenon construction, and small size are also characteristic of all the buildings. Al-

Moye Plantation.
Slave cabin.

Moye Plantation.
Interior detail of slave cabin.

Moye Plantation.
Interior window detail in the slave cabin.

Moye Plantation.
Detail of the fireplace, slave cabin.

though privies were common, the Moye privy is unique in that it is large (five-seat capacity), and the privy holes are of varying diameters. The size of the structure would certainly indicate that it was not intended for use by the owner's family.

Most of the outbuildings are in fair to good condition. Those in need of repair have received attention from the owner. The plantation remains a testimony to the love and care of six generations of the West-Moye family that have lived there.

Moye Plantation.
Detail of interior construction in the privy.

Moye Plantation.
The schoolhouse.

Moye Plantation.
The blacksmith's shop, rear view.

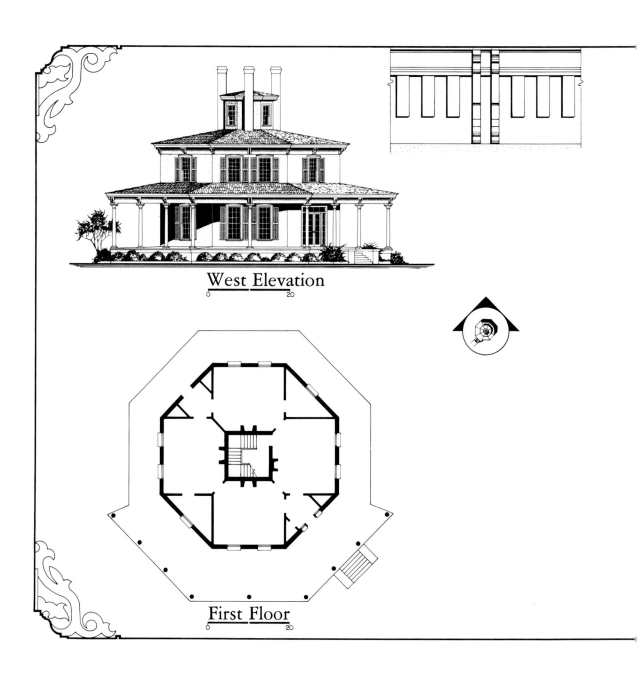

West Elevation

0   20

First Floor

0   20

Locally known as the Octagon House, the old Petty-Roberts home is one of the unusual structures in the Lower Chattahoochee Valley (Figure 54). Around 1850 the Octagon Fad erupted in the United States. Roofs were flat or low and often surmounted by a belvedere. It was common for houses to be surrounded by verandas with galleries above. Detail varied greatly from plain to elaborate Victorian motifs. Most octagon houses in the United States were built between 1848 and 1860. The style is attributed to the influence of a book by Orson Squire Fowler. According to Fowler, the advantage of the plan was maximum utilization of space. Houses of an octagon shape were built across

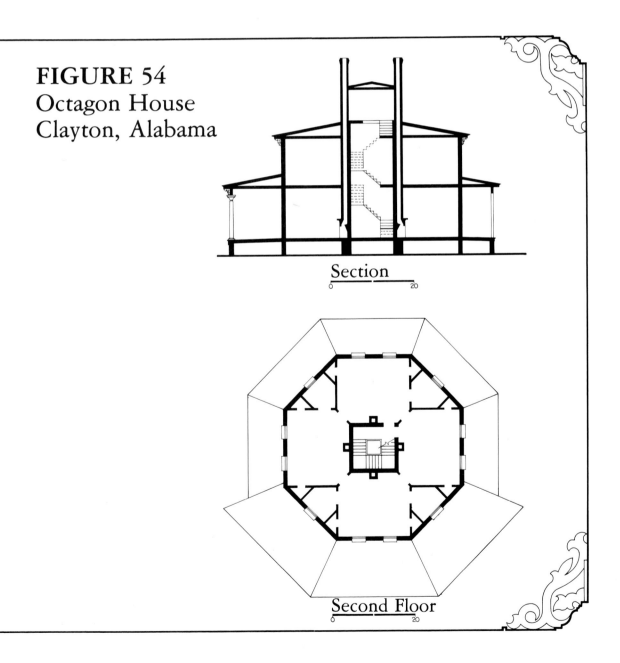

FIGURE 54
Octagon House
Clayton, Alabama

Section

Second Floor

the United States, but the northeastern sector appears to have been the core area.

The Petty-Roberts home was built between 1859 and 1861 for Mr. Benjamin Franklin Petty. Undoubtedly he was familiar with Fowler's designs in New York, Petty's home state. B. F. Petty settled in Clayton, Alabama, in 1835 and eventually married the daughter of Charles Lewis, one of the founding citizens of Barbour County. Petty's second wife was a granddaughter of Charles Lewis. The house was sold in 1899 to Leila Augusta and Nannie Allen Petty (Mrs. C. S. Herlong). In 1901 they in turn sold it to Claudia Roberts, the wife of Judge Bob T. Roberts. The house was inherited by Mary Roberts Beatty, their daughter, who married Elliott S. Armistead in 1971. Mr. Armistead has lived in the Octagon House since Mrs. Armistead's death in 1973.

Octagon House.
South elevation. The stairs were added in 1924.

Octagon House.
Detail of the porch and stairs.

Octagon House.
The basement entrance.

Octagon House.
Detail of construction.

The original floor plan showed four rooms upstairs and down, plus a full basement. Small, wedge-shaped rooms separated each of the eight rooms. Two of the lower floor corner rooms served as a front and rear vestibule. The stairwell has always been in the center of the house. In the full basement was space for the kitchen, dining room, and pantry. There was a long central hall down the middle of the basement, flanked by small rooms used for coal, wood, or general storage.

The house has undergone considerable alteration during its history. A significant change is in the former entrance vestibule, where a window has replaced the door; two windows in the left parlor have been transformed into doors. Upstairs, each of the wedge-shaped rooms has been altered to form a pentagon, with closets added in the small triangular spaces (see floor plan). With the addition of outside stairs in 1924, the corner room over the original entrance was changed to an entrance. A door was cut in the left wall of the new entrance foyer and a parlor made in the upper front room. The

Octagon House.
Framework in the cupola.

stairwell from the first to second floor was closed and the stairs removed. Modification of this lower stairwell area provided closets, bookshelves, and a general storage area. A second upstairs corner room became a kitchen.

Despite its numerous major alterations, the Octagon House has been lovingly cared for and has rightfully become something of a showplace for the citizens of Clayton. Because the Octagon Fad was short-lived, this example is of historical and architectural significance.

Octagon House.
Detail of the parlor mantel.

Octagon House.
An example of ceiling molding.

Octagon House.
Detail of parlor cornice.
Note the interior position of the chimney flue.

Russell County Courthouse.
West elevation.

Russell County Courthouse

The brick courthouse at Seale, Russell County, Alabama, is representative of a style known as Jeffersonian Classicism (Figure 55). The dominant white portico, use of Tuscan (Roman) columns, red brick, and a window or design in the pediment are defining characteristics. The plan of the Jeffersonian building is rectangular, and the general squareness is accentuated by straight-topped windows and low-pitched roofs.

County records are nonexistent prior to 1870. After Lee County was partially created from portions of Russell County in 1866, the legislature ordered an election to determine a more central location for the Russell County courthouse. Local government was considerably disrupted during Reconstruction, and records were improperly kept. Tradition holds that Silver Run (later Seale) won the election and construction of the courthouse com-

FIGURE 55
Russell County Courthouse
Seale, Alabama

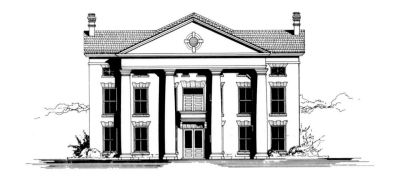

West Elevation

South Elevation

Second Floor Plan

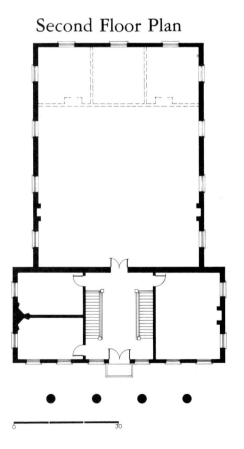

First Floor Plan

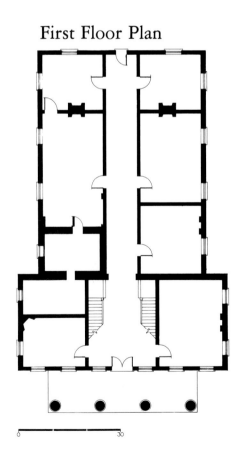

menced immediately. One of the sons of Ulysees Lewis (first mayor of Columbus, Georgia, and a founding citizen of Russell County) and Simeon O'Neal set about to build the structure. According to the latter's granddaughters, Emma Martin Chadwick and Lummie Hammons Holland, excavation began shortly after the election. Work was sporadic. Another election was held in 1868, and Seale won a second time. Once again Lewis and Simeon started working. They were not commissioned by a duly elected County Board of Commissioners until February 1870.

Until 1870, or perhaps later, Cicero McBride held the title to the courthouse property. The jail was completed in 1869 and the first floor of the courthouse in 1870. Not until 1871 was the building completed. It was used as the Russell County courthouse and branch courthouse until 1953. Many prominent Alabama lawyers and judges rose to fame from service in the Russell County structure. Among the more memorable were Aurelius Augustus Evans and James Billingslea Mitchell, who became members of the Alabama Supreme Court. Two other prominent lawyers were Colonel Lyman Waddell Martin and Major James Fleming Waddell.

The building was extensively remodeled in 1908 with the addition of the front lower and upper rooms and the stair hall; previously the stairs had been outside. The structure was rebricked in its entirety with commercially produced brick. The architect for the renovation was T. F. Lockwood of Columbus, Georgia. Although the old courthouse was abused and neglected for a number of years, a new era is dawning in its history. Efforts are under way to restore the structure for use as an office building and museum of Russell County history.

An imposing structure situated on top of a hill, the courthouse commands an impressive view. Constructed of red brick, walls are 15 inches thick, and interior surfaces are plaster over masonry. Interior details are lacking in parts of the building. Fireplaces are shallow, coal-burning types; there are no mantel details. Wainscoting is found only in the main entrance and is narrow-headed siding. The ceiling on the second floor is stamped metal tacked onto furring strips. Plans for offices and a museum are exemplary.

Russell County Courthouse.
Note the windows of the courtroom and the artistic brickwork in the chimney caps.

Russell County Courthouse.
Detail of the portico and Tuscan order columns.

Grave Shelters

The building of sheds, houses, or other protective cover for graves is a widespread and ancient cultural trait. It is one of the many aspects of human endeavor that brings forth the inevitable question: "Why?" The intriguing study of the cultural and geographic impact of cemeteries as a human use of the earth is in its infancy. Grave shelters represent but one element of a complex cultural association dealing with man's landscape expression of death.

Grave shelters illustrated here are typical of burial shelters previously widespread in the South. Interestingly enough, the grave shed does not appear to have been common outside the southeastern United States. Before analyzing the distribution of burial sheds, it is necessary to step back and consider some important aspects about cemetery monuments.

The simple shed shares a function similar to that of notable monuments to the dead. The most studied grave monuments in the world are the pyramids of Egypt. Famed for their gigantic proportions, they differ mainly in size from other grave houses. Smaller, more detailed and architecturally elaborate, grave houses can be observed in Russian Orthodox cemeteries in Alaska. The Catholic cemeteries of France, Italy, and southern Louisiana have many fine examples of "houses of the dead." What is the bridging link among these diverse examples? The answer remains elusive. Yet, all of these types of grave houses seem to share a common purpose—ultimately, to protect the grave. It may very well be that no continuous use of grave sheds has developed and that man has repeatedly "invented" the trait as the situation demanded.

Necrogeographical research conducted throughout the southeastern United States over the last ten years has resulted in some noteworthy observations about the American grave shelter. Burial coverings have been photographed or verified from more than 124 counties, extending from the valley of Texas and northern Mexico to Virginia. The sheds differ considerably in style, although all are of the same basic type—an open shed with a gabled roof supported by four corner posts. The gables are usually aligned with the grave, one at the head and one at the foot.

The use of grave sheds in America seems to have been most popular during the Victorian era, ca. 1840–1890. It is suggested that the more elaborate styles, especially, were an effort to mimic the grand examples of mausoleums in urban cemeteries of the eastern United States. The typical rural grave shed was wooden. Most were constructed of heart pine and fastened together using wooden pegs or hand-wrought nails. The roof was of shakes, although later substitution was commonly corrugated tin. Another stylistic feature was picket fencing.

Through the latter part of the nineteenth century, the grave shed underwent numerous style changes. Most changes were fancy trimwork. Picket fencing became very ornate. Scalloped trim was sometimes added to the eaves. Scalloped shakes were at times used. In the more elaborate forms, Victorian gingerbread adorned the gables.

The size of grave sheds is variable. Most recorded are single adult grave structures, approximately 5 feet x 7 feet. Similar structures over a child's grave have varied from 2 feet x 3 feet to the average adult size. Infrequently, a grave shed over two, possibly three, graves may be seen.

The reasons proffered for building grave covers has ranged from the sublime to the limits of reasonable acceptability. Surely a large factor was protection for the grave. In early settlements, cemeteries were not always fenced; roving farm animals, especially swine, posed a very real problem—not disturbance of the body, but damage to the surface of the grave. The logical solution was to put a fence around the grave. Such a measure also prevented cattle from trampling the grave sites.

A roof over the grave served another important function. Heavy rains in the southeastern and south central United States resulted in problems of erosion. Washing was common; the result was often unsightly, sunken graves and exposed coffins. Most graveyards contained a pile of dirt that could be used by families to fill and mound graves that had been eroded. Mounding each grave helped to lessen the problem, but it was not completely satisfactory. A better solution was to cover the grave with a small shed. In such a manner erosion and settling was seldom a problem. Why every family did not construct grave sheds must be attributed to the unpredictable behavior of humans. Some rural burial grounds were graced by a single shed while others had many.

Today, the grave shed has virtually disappeared from the American cemetery. As the sheds weaken and collapse, families seldom rebuild them. Scattered photographs, elderly folk with keen memories, and rare examples are all that remain of what was once a more common and widespread cultural feature. The American grave shelter stands as a reminder of the respect, practicability, and adaptability of our early forefathers. Each of the following examples is typical of this once pervasive cemetery feature.

The grave shelter at Liberty Methodist Church, Henry County, Alabama, (Figure 56) was built in 1909. It protects the grave of Mrs. Mary Dixon Scott who died in 1904. The shed

Liberty Methodist Church Grave Shelter.

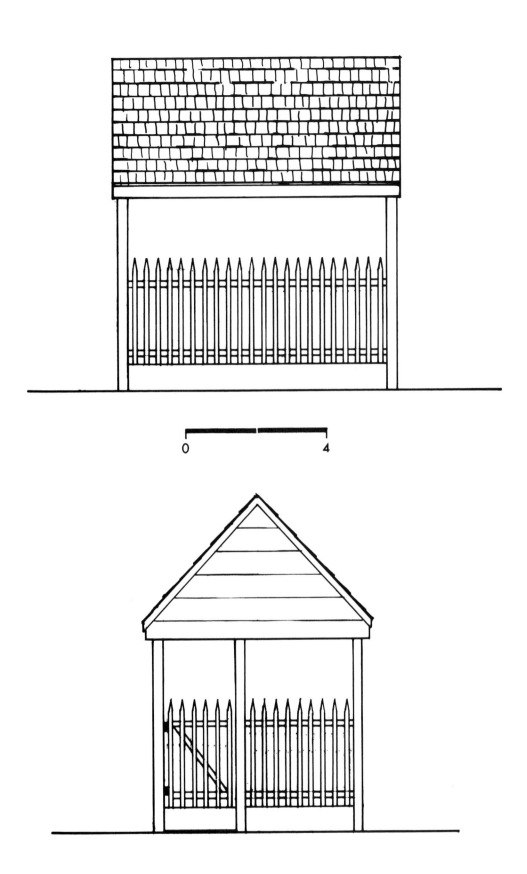

FIGURE 56
Liberty Methodist Church Grave Shelter
Henry County, Alabama

was constructed by her son-in-law, William Edwin Hudspeth, using heart pine, peg construction, and wooden shingles for the roof; it was painted white. The shelter was repaired by the Liberty United Methodist Youth Fellowship in March 1977, under the guidance of Mrs. Dorothy Powell. The picket fence and gable supports were in excellent condition. The rafters and wooden shingles had to be replaced. It is to be repainted white.

Liberty Methodist Church Grave Shelter.
Detail of the gate and latch.

The Bethany Baptist Church grave shed (Figure 57), in Harris County, Georgia, is one of the large, rarer types. It covers two graves, those of Elizabeth and David Jenkins; the latter died in 1870, the former in 1881. The shelter probably dates from Mrs. Jenkins's death. There seems to be little evidence of grave shelters being built to incorporate future burials. Another significant difference is that the graves are parallel to the gables rather than at right angles to them. The structure has an interesting serrated trim around the tops of the support posts. Except for a weak roof, the shelter appears to be in good condition.

FIGURE 57
Grave Shelter
Bethany Baptist Church
Harris County, Georgia

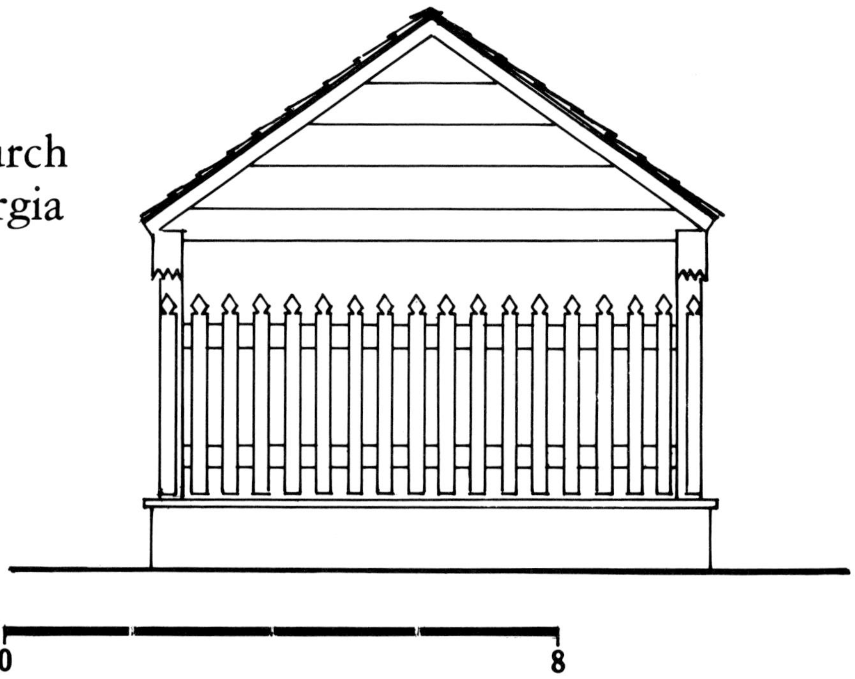

0   8

Stone inscriptions:
Elizabeth Jenkins, Born 1806, Died 1881
David Jenkins, Born 1804, Died 1870

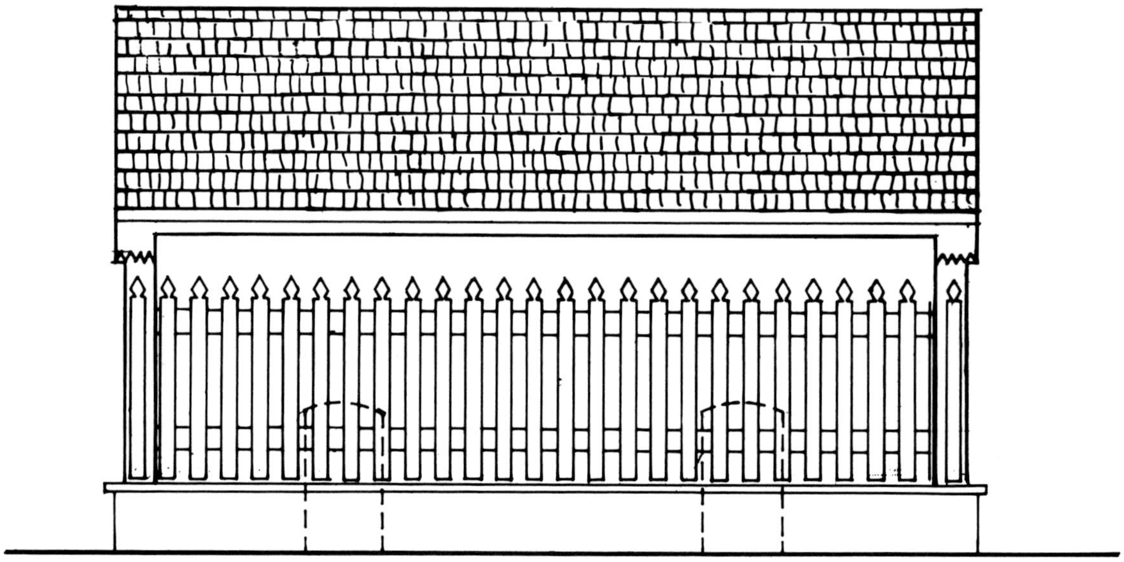

Bethany Baptist Church Grave Shelter.

Bethany Baptist Church Grave Shelter.
Detail of pickets and trim on support posts.

One of the more detailed and carefully constructed grave shelters is found in the Providence Chapel Cemetery at Red Hill, Stewart County, Georgia (Figure 58). The horizontal bracing is pegged into the posts (see detail in drawing). There is no stone or marker inside the shelter. All fascia and trim boards are mitered. The boxed eaves, the shingles on the gables, and the overall design are indicative of the craftsmanship. It is ornate in its own way, yet simple. The shelter's location in the cemetery next to Providence Chapel is of note. The chapel is on one of the earliest church sites in Georgia, dating back to 1837. Services were held in the early 1830s by Rev. George Lynch Smith, at first under a brush arbor and later in a log schoolhouse. The present chapel was erected in 1857.

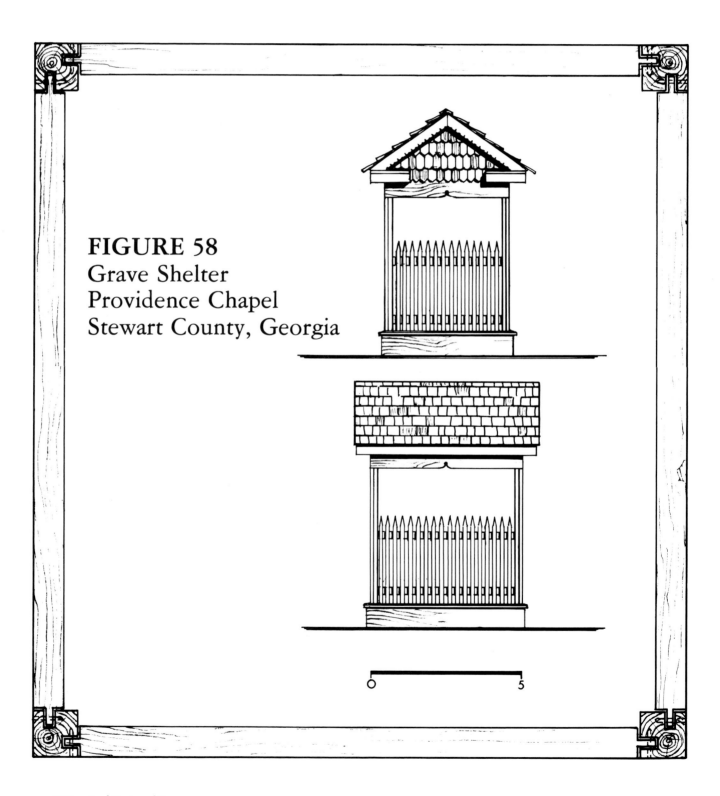

FIGURE 58
Grave Shelter
Providence Chapel
Stewart County, Georgia

0   5

Providence Chapel Grave Shelter.

Providence Chapel Grave Shelter.
Detail of the gable. Note the wooden shingles and the boxed eave.

The grave sheds at Mount Lebanon Baptist Church and the Hyram Cemetery, both in Russell County, Alabama, and the Antioch Methodist Church, in Lee County, Alabama,

FIGURE 59
Grave Shelters

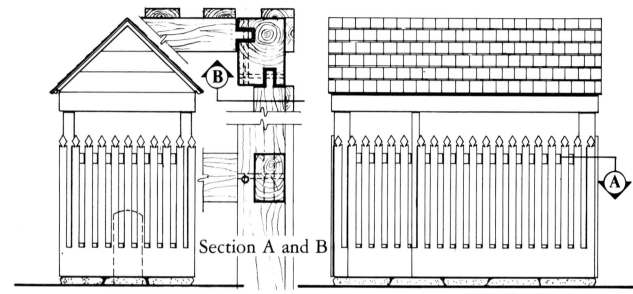

Section A and B

Mount Lebanon Baptist Church
Russell County, Alabama

Stone inscription:
Thomas Nelsen, Born March 25, 1814,
Died Oct. 25, 1862, 48 yrs. & 7 mos.

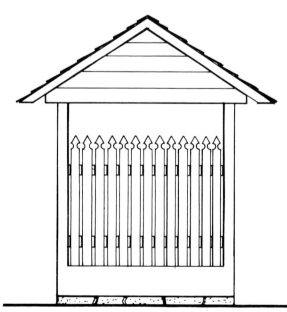

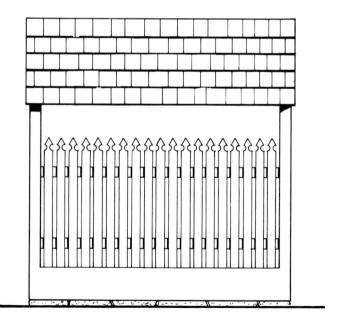

Antioch Methodist Church
Lee County, Alabama
Grave of Henry Prince

are all similar (Figure 59). The Mount Lebanon structure shows indications of peg construction. The shelter, in poor condition, covers a single grave, that of Thomas Nelson, who died

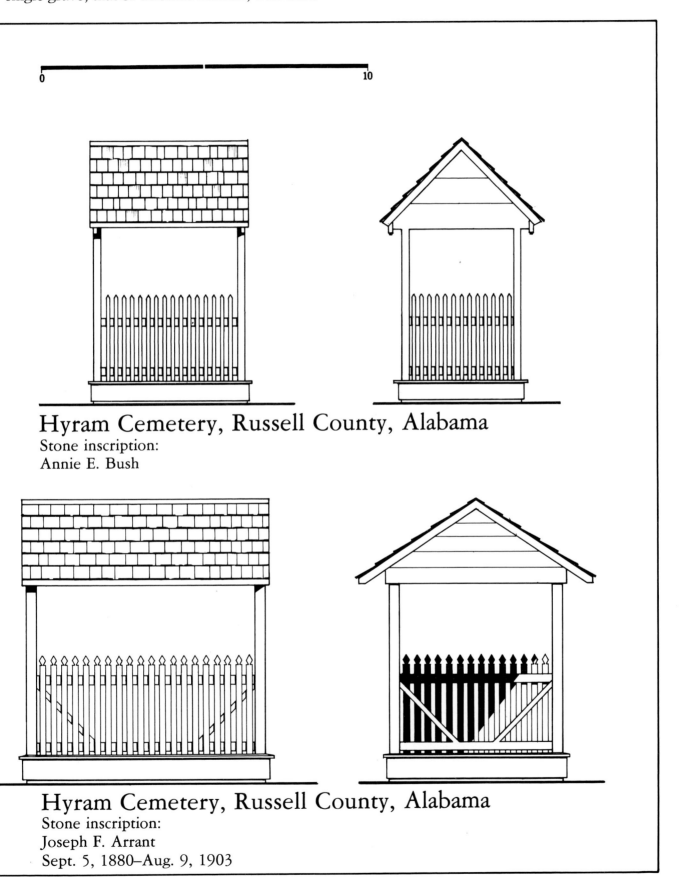

0   10

Hyram Cemetery, Russell County, Alabama
Stone inscription:
Annie E. Bush

Hyram Cemetery, Russell County, Alabama
Stone inscription:
Joseph F. Arrant
Sept. 5, 1880–Aug. 9, 1903

Mount Lebanon Baptist Church Grave Shelter.

Mount Lebanon Baptist Church Grave Shelter.
Detail of the gate latch.

in 1862. The grave of Henry Prince at Antioch Methodist Church cemetery is protected by a shelter that is in fair condition. The bracing for the shed is notched into the posts and pegged. The Prince family was an important old family in the area, and possibly the shelter dates from

Antioch Methodist Church Grave Shelter.

the Civil War era. The small shelter over Anne Bush's grave at Hyram is near collapse. The grave cover is typical of the region and is plain except for a tiny spindle at each eave corner. The braces are nailed into the posts indicating later construction than those pegged together. The larger Hyram shelter, protecting Joseph F. Arrant's grave, is also near collapse. It is somewhat unusual in that one end is open. Apparently, part of the picket fence rotted away. Braces are notched and pegged into the support posts. This particular shelter had a ceiling instead of the common mode of exposed rafters.

Hyram Grave Shelters.

Hyram Grave Shelter.
Detail of shingle roof.

The grave shelter at Crawford, Russell County, Alabama, is an elaborate structure as these sheds go (Figure 60). The shed is in good condition. Columns rest on a full perimeter brick coping. Considerable attention went into constructing this cover. There is a fair amount of Victorian ornamentation as evidenced by brackets and spindles. The Eastlake-style wooden rosette can be found on the brackets.

The shelter has a ceiling of beaded tongue and groove lumber similar to that used as wainscoting in so many Victorian homes. Although large and open, the shelter protects only one grave, whose stone inscription is for Mrs. A. J. Stripling. Adjoining her plot, but uncovered, are the graves of G. W. Gullatte and Mrs. Jane Gullatte. All these graves are in the same fenced enclosure; the connection is unknown.

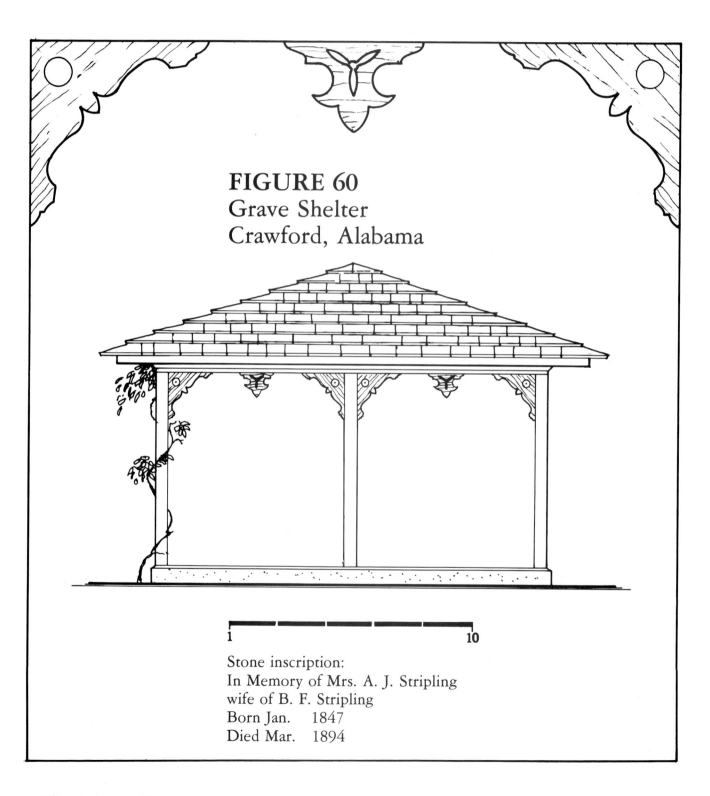

FIGURE 60
Grave Shelter
Crawford, Alabama

1   10

Stone inscription:
In Memory of Mrs. A. J. Stripling
wife of B. F. Stripling
Born Jan.   1847
Died Mar.   1894

Crawford Grave Shelter.

Crawford Grave Shelter.
Detail of the Victorian trim.

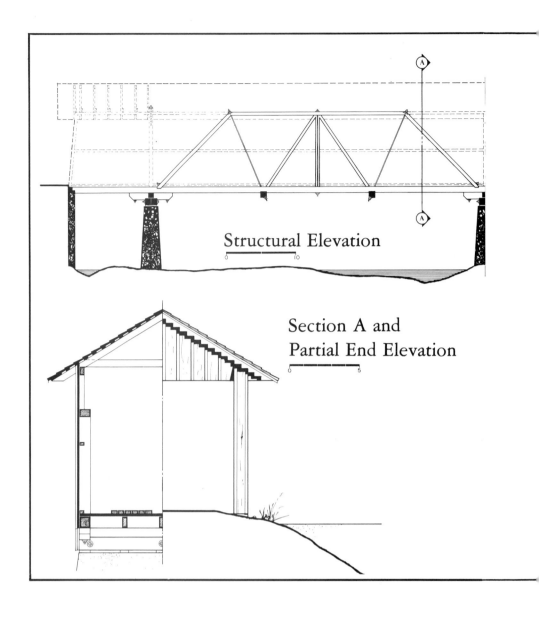

Structural Elevation

Section A and
Partial End Elevation

Coheelee Creek Bridge

Situated in Early County, Georgia, nine miles southwest of Blakely, in Hilton, is a unique structure for the Lower Chattahoochee Valley, the covered bridge over Coheelee Creek (Figure 61). The unique feature is that it is the southernmost bridge of its kind in the United States. The bridge was built across the creek in 1891 at a point known as McDonald's Ford. It is erroneously listed as being constructed in 1883 by Richard S. Allen in his *Covered Bridges of the South.* Apparently, the error was made in reading the minutes of the Commissioner's Court.

The first reference to the covered bridge is in 1883 when a committee composed of J. S. Mosely, W. C. Sheffield, H. C. Fryer, and J. P. Pane was authorized to inquire into the practi-

Partial West Elevation

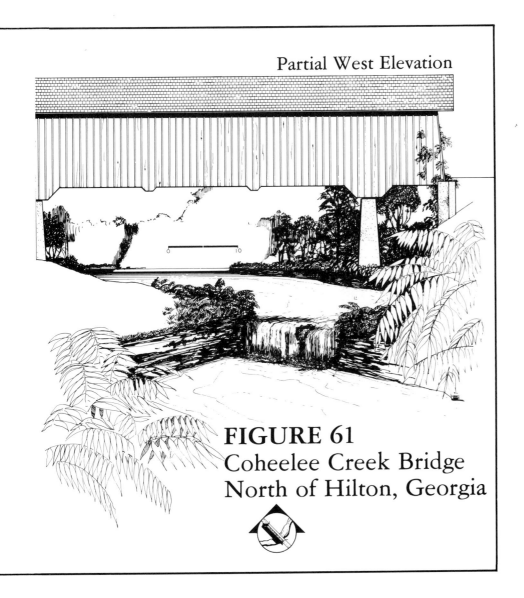

FIGURE 61
Coheelee Creek Bridge
North of Hilton, Georgia

Coheelee Creek Bridge.

cality of constructing a bridge across the Coheelee at McDonald's Ford. The site was passed up in favor of one across Sowhatchee Creek a bit farther south. Eight years passed before the commission finally got around to building a bridge over Coheelee. Minutes from the meeting of July 7, 1891, authorize payment for labor on four bridges: Damascus, Howard's Mill, Singletary's Mill, and Coheelee Creek. The supervisor who paid for "expenses of Bridge at Cowheely Creek" was J. W. Baughman. J. B. Mosely was foreman. In addition, a long list of workers with their respective wages was included. The following workmen helped build the covered bridge: P. L. Howard, Ira Martin, C. H. Gray, Guss Jackson, Lee McDonald, Guss Davison, J. N. Pyle, D. G. Moulton, P. C. Johnson, Jim Golden, Tom Holton, Bery Scarbaugh, George Harris, Mose Hollinger, Will Holmes, Collins Bendross, Lewis Bowell, Babe Chambers, W. W. Weaver, Tom Chambers, and Josh Perry. Other laborers

Coheelee Creek Bridge.
Detail of the truss.

were added from time to time. The fate of the Coheelee bridge remains a question.

The bridge is still in fair to good condition. The core is a king post truss with supporting 1½ inch diameter metal rods, called tension rods. The concrete piers are additions; the originals probably were of stone. Little of the original siding remains; the vertical siding was 1 x 12 inch pine with 1 x 3 inch batten strips. The roof system has been completely replaced (the drawing shows the new system). The weight of any load on the bridge is borne by the truss; the dotted lines in the drawing indicate nonbearing framing used for siding.

The covered bridge is adjacent to the Fannie Askew Williams Park, maintained by the county. Land for the park was donated by the late John H. Williams of Blakely in 1959. Location off the beaten path has preserved this structure for the pleasure of many. One can only hope it will continue to bring pleasure in the future.

Coheelee Creek Bridge.
Detail of the substructure.

SPECIAL ACKNOWLEDGMENTS

The following lists for Alabama and Georgia include the names of individuals who so graciously gave of their time, money, or knowledge to make this project a success. The format is to list the county and each structure from that county. Under each structure is the name of the persons responsible for our information. Because some people helped with more than one structure, their names may appear a number of times. It is sincerely hoped that no person has been omitted; if so, the editors extend their apology.

Alabama

BARBOUR COUNTY

Alexander Home: Mr. Capers Alexander, Batesburg, South Carolina; Mr. William L. Cawthon, Smyrna, Georgia; Mr. William L. Cawthon, Jr., Macon, Georgia; Mr. Humphrey Foy, Eufaula, Alabama; Mr. Ross Foy, Eufaula, Alabama.

Barbour County High School: The George C. Wallace Heritage Association, Clio, Alabama; Mr. Alto L. Jackson, Clio, Alabama; Mr. Sam W. Jackson, Clio, Alabama; Mrs. C. A. Laird (Mildred T.).

Octagon House and **Jennings House:** Mr. Elliott S. Armistead, Clayton, Alabama; Barbour County Historical Society, Clayton, Alabama; Mr. William Oates Caraway, Clayton, Alabama; Clayton Heritage Association, Clayton, Alabama; Mr. Bart Jennings, Jr., Mobile, Alabama; Mr. Bruce Jennings, Mobile, Alabama; Mrs. Sharon Martin (John C. II), Clayton, Alabama; Mr. Charles Weston, Clayton, Alabama.

Vicksburg and Brunswick Depot: Eufaula Heritage Association, Eufaula, Alabama; Mr. Milo B. Howard, Jr., Montgomery, Alabama; Mr. Mac Mitchell, Eufaula, Alabama; Mr. Douglas Clare Purcell, Eufaula, Alabama; Mrs. Florence Foy Strang, Eufaula, Alabama.

CHAMBERS COUNTY

Barrow Home and **Trammell Home:** Mrs. Marjorie Andrews, Lafayette, Alabama; Chattahoochee Valley Historical Society, West Point, Georgia; Mr. William Davidson, West Point, Georgia; Dr. David M. Hall, Auburn, Alabama; Mr. John Harris, Mrs. Eleanor Harris (John), Cusseta, Alabama; Mr. Alvin Phillips, Lafayette, Alabama; Mr. Charles H. Weissinger, Opelika, Alabama.

DALE COUNTY

Dowling-Holman Home: Dale County Historical Society, Ozark, Alabama; Mrs. Margaret Steagall Holman, Ozark, Alabama.

HENRY COUNTY

Kennedy Home: Abbeville Community Improvement Council, Abbeville, Alabama; Henry County Board of Education, Abbeville, Alabama; Henry County Historical Society, Abbeville, Alabama; Mr. William W. Nordan, Abbeville, Alabama; Mrs. Verna Nordan Owens, Abbeville, Alabama.

Liberty Methodist Church Grave Shelter: Dr. Gregory Jeane, Opelika, Alabama; Liberty United Methodist Youth Fellowship, Abbeville, Alabama; Mrs. W. V. Powell (Dorothy), Abbeville, Alabama.

Mills House, Gray House, Pelham House, Saddlebag House, Graham House: Mr. C. W. Mills, Shorterville, Alabama; Dr. Eugene Wilson, Mobile, Alabama.

HOUSTON COUNTY

Columbia Jailhouse: Mrs. Connie Brodzinski, Columbia, Alabama; Columbia Bicentennial Committee, Columbia, Alabama; Mrs. Sandra Gray, Columbia, Alabama; Haleburg Historical Society, Columbia, Alabama; Mrs. Viola H. Oakley (M. L.), Columbia, Alabama; Mrs. Mary Carol Ward, Columbia, Alabama; Mr. Fred S. Watson, Dothan, Alabama; Wiregrass Historical Society, Dothan, Alabama.

LEE COUNTY

Antioch Methodist Church Grave Shelter: Dr. Gregory Jeane, Opelika, Alabama.

Edwards Home: Miss Sarah Lula Bean, Opelika, Alabama; Mr. Charles H. Weissinger, Opelika, Alabama.

Gold Hill Commissary: Dr. Gregory Jeane, Opelika Alabama; Mr. George Robertson, Jr., Gold Hill, Alabama; Mr. George Robertson, Sr., Gold Hill, Alabama; Mr. Charles H. Weissinger, Opelika, Alabama.

Meadows Mill: Mrs. Hugh Byrd, Auburn, Alabama; Lee County Historical Society, Loachapoka, Alabama; Mr. W. T. Ingram, Auburn, Alabama; Professor O. T. Ivey, Auburn, Alabama; Dr. Gregory Jeane, Opelika, Alabama; Dr. Alexander Nunn, Loachapoka, Alabama; Mr. G. L. Story, Salem, Alabama; Dr. H. Floyd Vallery, Auburn, Alabama.

Neva Winston House: Auburn Heritage Association, Auburn, Alabama; Mrs. Jan Dempsey, Auburn, Alabama; Mrs. Alice Cary Pick Gibson, Auburn, Alabama; Dr. Gregory Jeane, Opelika, Alabama; Dr. H. Floyd Vallery, Auburn, Alabama; Mr. Charles H. Weissinger, Opelika, Alabama.

RUSSELL COUNTY

Christian Log House: Mr. Louis Denson, Russell County; Mrs. Gertha Mae Holmes, Pittsview, Alabama; Mrs. Florence Foy Strang, Eufaula, Alabama; Dr. Eugene Wilson, Mobile, Alabama.

Crawford Grave Shelter: Dr. Gregory Jeane, Opelika, Alabama.

Goodhope Baptist Church: Peter A. Brannon, Montgomery, Alabama; Reuben Long Chapter DAR, Russell County, Alabama; Mr. K. Charles Tigner, Seale, Alabama; Mrs. Guy Vining (Sarah), Hurtsboro, Alabama; Mr. Cecial Williamson, Uchee, Alabama.

Hyram Grave Shelters (2): Dr. Gregory Jeane, Opelika, Alabama; Mr. K. Charles Tigner, Seale, Alabama.

Mitchell-Ferrell Home and **Russell County Courthouse:** Fort Mitchell Historical Society, Fort Mitchell, Alabama; Old Russell County Courthouse Association, Seale, Alabama; Russell County Historical Commission, Seale, Alabama; Mr. K. Charles Tigner, Seale, Alabama.

Mount Lebanon Baptist Church Grave Shelter: Dr. Gregory Jeane, Opelika, Alabama.

Uchee Methodist Church: Mr. Peter Brannon, Montgomery, Alabama; Mrs. Frank Persons, Uchee, Alabama.

Georgia

CHATTAHOOCHEE COUNTY

Liberty Hill Methodist Church: Mr. George R. McGlaun, Jr., Buena Vista, Georgia; Mrs. Marian M. McGlaun (George R., Sr.), Cusseta, Georgia.

CLAY COUNTY

Dill House: Mr. Jimmy Coleman, Fort Gaines, Georgia; Fort Gaines City Council, Fort Gaines, Georgia; Fort Gaines Historical Society, Fort Gaines, Georgia; Mr. P. C. King, Jr., Fort Gaines, Georgia; Mr. Jim Waters, Fort Gaines, Georgia; Mr. Robert Watson, Fort Gaines, Georgia.

DECATUR COUNTY

Coleman-Vickers Home and **Malone Stone House:** Mrs. Victoria C. Custer, Bainbridge, Georgia; Decatur County Historical Society, Bainbridge, Georgia; Mr. Sidney R. Mullen, Eufaula, Alabama; Mr. Maston E. O'Neal, Jr., Bainbridge, Georgia; Katherine Chesnut Wimberley, Bainbridge, Georgia.

EARLY COUNTY

Coheelee Creek Bridge: Early County Historical Society, Blakely, Georgia; Mr. Mobley Howell, Blakely, Georgia; Mr. Marvin Singletary, Blakely, Georgia; Mrs. Mary Grist Whitehead (Mrs. Ernest Pace), Blakely, Georgia.

HARRIS COUNTY

Bethany Baptist Church Grave Shelter: Mr. William Davidson, West Point, Georgia; Dr. Gregory Jeane, Opelika, Alabama.

Cleaveland-Godwin-Nelson-Peacock House: Chattahoochee Valley Historical Society, West Point, Georgia; Mr. William Davidson, West Point, Georgia; Mr. Edward W. Neal, Columbus, Georgia; Mr. J. D. Peacock, Columbus, Georgia.

William Walker-Cook-Hood House: Mr. William Davidson, West Point, Georgia; Mr. Edward W. Neal, Columbus, Georgia.

MUSCOGEE COUNTY

Special credit to the West Georgia Chapter, American Institute of Architects, and the Historic Columbus Foundation for all Muscogee County Structures.

Bullard-Hart Home: Mrs. Janice Biggers (Mrs. James J. W.), Columbus, Georgia; Hecht and Burdeshaw Architects, Columbus, Georgia; Mr. John Henry, Columbus, Georgia; Dr. and Mrs. Lloyd Sampson, Columbus, Georgia; Mrs. T. Earl Taylor, Jr. (Beverly), Columbus, Georgia.

Hoxey Home: Mrs. Janice Biggers (Mrs. James J. W.), Columbus, Georgia; Mr. Lloyd G. Bowers, III, Columbus, Georgia; Pound, Flowers, and Dedwylder Architects, Columbus, Georgia; Mrs. T. Earl Taylor, Jr. (Beverly), Columbus, Georgia.

Tingle Home: Mrs. Janice Biggers (Mrs. James J. W.), Columbus, Georgia; Biggers, Scarbrough, Neal, Crisp, and Clark Architects, Columbus, Georgia; Mrs. T. Earl Taylor, Jr. (Beverly), Columbus, Georgia.

Woolfolk Home: Mrs. Janice Biggers (Mrs. James J. W.), Columbus, Georgia; Biggers, Scarbrough, Neal, Crisp, and Clark Architects, Columbus, Georgia; Columbus Area Bicentennial Committee, Columbus, Georgia; Mrs. T. Earl Taylor, Jr. (Beverly), Columbus, Georgia.

QUITMAN COUNTY

Quitman County Jail: Mrs. Henry Balkcom, Jr. (Hortense), Georgetown, Georgia; City of Georgetown, Georgia; Quitman County Commission, Georgetown, Georgia; Mrs. W. Norton Roberts, Georgetown, Georgia.

RANDOLPH COUNTY

Hood Law Office and Key Gazebo-Greenhouse: Mr. Tommy Barr, Cuthbert, Georgia; Mr. Bobby Lovett, Cuthbert, Georgia; Randolph Historical Society, Cuthbert, Georgia; Mrs. T. N. Stapleton, Cuthbert, Georgia.

SEMINOLE COUNTY

Sikes-George House: Donalsonville-Seminole County Chamber of Commerce, Donalsonville, Georgia; Mr. C. G. George, Dothan, Alabama; Mrs. Mildred Johnson, Dothan, Alabama; Mrs. Marion Roberts, Donalsonville, Georgia; Mrs. John Ray Stout, Donalsonville, Georgia; Mrs. Julian Webb, Donalsonville, Georgia.

STEWART COUNTY

Moye Plantation Outbuildings: Mr. L. M. Moye, Lumpkin, Georgia.

Wood's Home: Brown's Guide to Georgia, College Park, Georgia; Mr. James A. Harrell, Columbus, Georgia; Mr. George Lee, Omaha, Georgia; Mrs. Ann Singer (Sam S.), Lumpkin, Georgia; Stewart County Historical Commission, Lumpkin, Georgia.

TROUP COUNTY

Frost-Gray Home: Mr. Thomas Lowe, Jr., Atlanta, Georgia; Henry and Catherine Tucker, LaGrange, Georgia.

Rutledge House: Atlanta Journal and Constitution; Brown's Guide to Georgia, College Park, Georgia; Callaway Foundation, LaGrange, Georgia (Callaway Foundation grant was used for all Georgia structures in Endangered Valley Structure Project); Chattahoochee Valley Historical Society, West Point, Georgia; Mrs. Jenny Copeland (Robert), LaGrange, Georgia; Mrs. Mary Jane Crayton, LaGrange, Georgia; Mr. William Davidson, West Point, Georgia; Mr. Gaston Hester, Eufaula, Alabama; Mr. Charles Hudson, LaGrange, Georgia; Ocfuskee Historical Society, LaGrange, Georgia.

GLOSSARY

acanthus A popular ornamentation of the Greek Revival period, representing the leaves of the acanthus plant, and used abundantly on the capitals of Corinthian columns.

Adam style A style of architecture characterized by lightness and delicacy, named for three brothers who had the largest architectural practice in England between 1760 and 1780.

alcove A recessed part of a room.

anthemion A flattened design of flowers or leaves patterned in a spreading cluster, used in art.

apse A circular, often vaulted or domed, end of a church, containing the altar.

arch A curved series of wedge-shaped blocks over an opening.

architrave The lowermost section of an entablature.

ashlar A squared stone used in building; or, masonry consisting of such stones.

attic An uppermost story or room, immediately below the roof of a building.

balloon framing A type of timber framing in which the studs run from sill to roof line without horizontal supports for floor joists.

baluster A small post supporting the railing of a staircase.

baseboard A board used to conceal the contact between an interior wall and the floor of a room. Its purpose is to add a finished look to the carpentry.

batten A narrow strip of wood used to cover the joint between two vertical boards.

bay window A window or windows projecting from a wall and from a ground foundation.

beveled Inclined at an angle or slanted.

boxed eaves Eaves that make a partial return at a gable.

bracket A projection used as decoration under an eave.

cantilever A projecting beam affixed only at one end, used architecturally in balconies and stairs.

capital The top part of a column or pilaster.

chair rail A molded strip of wood placed on a wall as a protection against chair backs.

clapboard A narrow board with one edge thicker than the other, overlapped to form weatherproof siding for exterior walls.

colonnade A row of columns.

common bond A type of brick bonding system in which every sixth row is a header row (ends) separated by horizontal rows (stretchers) of bricks.

coping The top part of a wall or roof.

Corinthian order The most elaborate of the Greek orders of architecture, characterized by slender columns with fluting and bell-shaped capitals ornamented with acanthus motifs.

cornice The top part of an entablature, resting on the frieze; the molding around the top of the walls of a room. See **crown molding.**

covenanter door See **Cross-and-Open-Bible door.**

Cross-and-Open-Bible door A type of door with six panels. The upper four panels form a cross; the lowest two represent an open Bible.

crown molding The molding placed around the contact between walls and ceilings. Sometimes called a *cornice.*

cupola A small room or structure on top of a roof.

cyma A type of S-shaped molding for a cornice.

dentil One of a series of small blocks that form a molding or projection beneath a cornice, usually on an entablature, although it may be found on the heavy interior cornice treatment of some Georgian architecture.

dogtrot A type of folk house characterized by two nearly equal rooms separated by an open, central passage and covered with one roof; also refers to the open passage.

Doric order The oldest and simplest of the Greek orders of architecture, characterized by heavy, fluted columns and simple capitals and cornices.

dormer A small gable-end window projecting from a sloping roof.

double pen A type of log folk house consisting of two butted rooms, usually having outside, gable-end chimneys and two front entrances.

dovetailing In folk architecture, a technique of notching logs that produces a tight interlocking joint when fitted into a similarly notched log. The fan-shaped log ends suggest the tail of a dove. (See drawings below.)

eaves The edge of a roof that projects over an outside wall.

egg and dart A molding in classical architecture consisting of a series of alternating egg-shaped and dart-shaped figures.

English one-bay house An early house type built by British immigrants in America. It usually was a single room (bay) with a fireplace on the inside of a gable-end wall. Additions were made by adding a bay to the gable-end opposite the fireplace or by adding the room to the rear of the house, forming an ell.

entablature In classical architecture, the horizontal superstructure resting on the column capital, divided into three major parts: architrave, frieze, and cornice.

facade The face of a building.

fanlight A fan-shaped window, usually above a door or large window.

fascia A flat horizontal band between moldings, commonly found in the architrave of a classical entablature.

SPECIAL METHODS
OF WALL BUILDING*

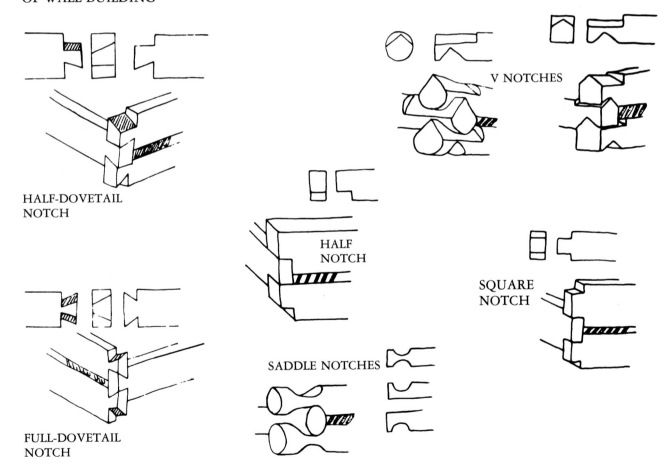

HALF-DOVETAIL NOTCH

FULL-DOVETAIL NOTCH

V NOTCHES

HALF NOTCH

SADDLE NOTCHES

SQUARE NOTCH

*Courtesy of Milton B. Newton, Jr., *Atlas of Louisiana: A Guide for Students,* Published by the School of Geoscience, Louisiana State University, Misc. Pub. 72-1, 1972.

Federal style See **Adam style.**

flush siding Boards nailed horizontally on a wall without overlapping so that the surface is smooth.

fluting Vertical grooves on a column, usually associated with the Doric order, though present in others.

four over four A common Southern floor plan in Greek Revival buildings, characterized by four rooms on each of two floors with a central hall on each floor.

fret An ornamental pattern of repeated, often symmetrical figures or lines within a band or border, sometimes referred to as the Greek key pattern.

fretwork Ornamental work consisting of frets in relief; geometric work or openwork popular on the gables of Victorian houses.

frieze A horizontal band, as the second part of an entablature between the cornice and architrave; also a strip along the upper part of a wall in a room.

gable The upper part of an outside end wall under the ridge of a steeply sloping roof.

gazebo A small pavilion, usually set in a formal garden.

Georgian style A style of English architecture popular during the eighteenth century, characterized by porchless facade, central hall, and symmetry in plan.

Greek Revival An architectural style popular in America between 1790 and about 1850, characterized by the use of classical Greek motifs, symmetry, and massiveness.

hall-and-parlor house An early British house type having external chimneys at each gable-end and an asymmetrical, two-room plan. Many were later built with a central hall as in the Georgian style.

I beam A beam or girder that resembles the capital letter I in cross section.

I house An English house type popular in the South, characterized by two stories, two rooms wide with a central hall, one room deep, and outside gable-end chimneys.

Jeffersonian Classicism An American architectural style with a heavy, massive effect, popular between 1780 and 1820, and characterized by the use of red bricks with a white portico of Tuscan order or unfluted Doric columns.

joist A horizontal beam supporting the boards of a floor or ceiling.

kingpost truss The simplest and first truss used in covered bridges in America, consisting of a center upright (kingpost) in the middle of the span, with two compression pieces slanting downward and outward toward each shore.

lath A thin riblike support of wood upon which plaster is spread.

loft An attic, usually not divided into rooms.

mansard A roof sloping twice on each of the four sides, with the lower slope nearly vertical, and the upper nearly horizontal.

mausoleum A large, imposing tomb.

medallion An oval or circular ceiling decoration, usually from which a light fixture is hung.

miter The diagonal joint formed by the edges of two pieces of molding or lumber meeting at right angles.

molding A decorative strip of wood or other material used to finish a wall or other surface.

mortise A space cut into a structural support and shaped to receive a corresponding tenon.

motif A distinctive, repeated figure in architectural decoration.

newel post The post supporting the handrail of a staircase.

parquetry Wood inlaid in decorative patterns in floors and furniture.

pediment A triangular gable on the facade of a building.

pier An upright wall or column used as a principal support.

pilaster A rectangular column attached to a wall.

portico A porch with columns supporting the roof.

post and lintel construction Construction with upright supports bearing beams (lintels). Usually refers to the Greek Revival window and door treatment.

pyramidal roof A roof having the shape of a pyramid, with all sides meeting to form a pointed peak or a truncated top.

pressed metal ceiling A decorative ceiling popular in the Victorian era, consisting of thin metal plates, often tin, embossed with a design.

ridge The top horizontal member of a sloping roof, stretching from gable to gable, against which the upper ends of rafters are attached.

riser The vertical part of a stair step.

rosette A circular ornament with parts painted or sculptured to suggest a rose.

saddlebag house A folk house type characterized by joining two rooms by a single central chimney with a room on each side.

scallop One of a series of semicircles or curves forming a decorative edge.

shed room A room with a sloping, one-sided roof, attached to the side or rear of a house.

shiplap Wooden boarding with the edges grooved so that each board overlaps the one below it.

sidelight A very narrow window flanking a door.

sill A horizontal beam supporting a vertical partition, such as a wall.

single pen A folk house type characterized by one room with an outside, gable-end chimney, similar to the English one-bay house.

soffit The exposed undersurface of any overhead part of a building, such as an eave, arch, beam, or doorhead.

square notch A type of log notch in which the lower half of the end of a log is cut out. When placed on top of other logs, it forms a square corner with no log overhang. (See drawing on p. 271.)

stone crane A special crane used in a mill to lift the grinding stones for sharpening.

stucco A durable coating for exterior or interior walls, usually made of cement, sand, and lime.

tenon A projection on the end of a piece of wood shaped to fit into a corresponding mortise to form a joint.

tongue and groove A type of joint where a continuous ridge of wood on one edge of a board is inserted into a corresponding groove on an adjacent board. Each board has a tongue, or a ridge of wood, on one edge and a groove on the other.

trabeated construction A type of Greek construction technique where the beam (lintel) is the dominant feature, as opposed to the use of the arch.

transom A small window above a door, usually hinged, on interior doors.

truss A framework of beams supporting a bridge, roof, or other structure.

Tuscan order A classical order of architecture, characterized by unfluted columns with simplified bases, capitals, and entablatures. It is the Roman equivalent of the Greek Doric order.

veranda A porch, usually roofed and often partly enclosed, extending along the outside of a building.

vestibule A small entrance hall or antechamber.

wainscot A facing, usually of wood paneling, on the lower part of the walls of a room.

SELECTED BIBLIOGRAPHY

Addy, Sidney O. *The Evolution of the English House.* London: Swan Sonnenschein and Co., 1898.

Allen, Richard Sanders. *Covered Bridges of the South.* New York: Bonanza Books, 1970.

Arthur, Eric and Dudley Witney. *The Barn: A Vanishing Landmark in North America.* Toronto: M. F. Feheley Arts Co., 1972.

Benjamin, Asher. *The American Builder's Companion.* Boston: R. P. and C. Williams at Dutton and Wentworth, Printers, 1827. Dover paperback edition, 1969.

Bicknell, A. J. *Victorian Village Builder.* Published for The Athenaeum Library of Nineteenth Century America. Watkins Glen, New York: The American Life Foundation, 1976.

Bullock, Orin M., Jr. *The Restoration Manual.* Norwalk, Connecticut: Silvermine Publishers, 1966.

Bye, Ranulph. *The Vanishing Depot.* Wynnewood, Pennsylvania: Livingston Publishing Co., 1973.

Davidson, William H. *Pine Log and Greek Revival.* Alexander City, Alabama: Outlook Publishing Co., 1964.

Detail, Cottage and Constructive Architecture. New York: A. J. Bicknell and Co., 1873.

Downing, Andrew Jackson. *Cottage Residences.* New York: John Wiley and Sons, 1887; *The Architecture of Country Houses.* New York: D. Appleton and Co., 1850. Dover paperback edition, 1969.

Eastlake, Charles L. *A History of the Gothic Revival.* Watkins Glen, New York: American Life Foundation, 1975. Reprint of the 1872 edition. See also *Hints on Household Taste.* London: Longman, Green and Co., 1878. Dover paperback edition, 1969.

Fitch, James Marston. *American Building: The Historical Forces that Shaped It.* 2nd Ed. New York: Schocken Books, 1973.

Foreman, Henry Chandler. *The Architecture of the Old South: The Medieval Style, 1585–1850.* Cambridge: Harvard University Press, 1948.

Gillon, Edmund V., Jr. *Early Illustrations and Views of American Architecture.* New York: Dover Publications, 1971.

Gillon, Edmund V., Jr. and Clay Lancaster. *Victorian Houses: A Treasury of Lesser Known Examples.* New York: Dover Publications, 1973.

Glassie, Henry. *Pattern in the Material Folk Culture of the Eastern United States.* Philadelphia: University of Pennsylvania Press, 1968.

Hamlin, Talbot. *Greek Revival Architecture in America.* New York: Oxford University Press, 1944. Dover paperback edition, 1964.

Klamkin, Charles. *Barns.* New York: Hawthorn Books, 1973.

Kniffen, Fred B. "Folk Housing: Key to Diffusion," *Annals,* Association of American Geographers, Vol. 55, No. 4 (December, 1965), pp. 549–77; "Louisiana House Types," *Annals,* Association of American Geographers, Vol. 26, No. 4 (December, 1936), pp. 179–93.

Lancaster, Clay. *New York Interiors at the Turn of the Century.* New York: Dover Publications, 1976.

Lewis, Arnold and Keith Morgan. *American Victorian Architecture: A Survey of the 70's and 80's in Contemporary Photographs.* New York: Dover Publications, 1975.

Linley, John. *Architecture of Middle Georgia: The Oconee Area.* Athens: University of Georgia Press, 1972.

McKee, Harley J. *Introduction to Early American Masonry.* Washington, D.C.: National Trust for Historic Preservation, 1973.

Modern Architectural Designs and Details. New York: William T. Comstock and Co., 1881.

Palliser's New Cottage Homes. New York: Palliser, Palliser and Co., 1887.

Peterson, Charles E. (Ed.). *Building Early America: Contributions Toward the History of a Great Industry.* Radnor, Pennsylvania: Chilton Book Co. Commemorating the 250th Anniversary of the Carpenters' Company of the City and County of Pennsylvania.

Seale, William. *The Tasteful Interlude: American Interiors Through the Camera's Eye, 1860–1917.* New York: Praeger Publishers, 1975.

Sloane, Eric. *American Barns and Covered Bridges.* New York: Funk and Wagnalls, 1954; *A Museum of Early American Tools.* New York: Ballantine Books, 1964; *A Reverence for Wood.* New York: Ballantine Books, 1965; *An Age of Barns.* New York: Ballantine Books, 1967.

Smith, J. Frazer. *White Pillars.* New York: William Helburn, 1941.

Stokes, George A. "Lumbering in Southwest Louisiana: A Study of the Industry as a Culture-Geographic Factor." (Ph.D. dissertation, Louisiana State University, 1954).

Victorian Architecture: Two Pattern Books by A. J. Bicknell and W. T. Comstock. Watkins Glen, New York: American Life Foundation, 1975.

Waite, Diana S. (Ed.). *Architectural Elements: The Technological Revolution.* New York: Bonanza Books. n.d.

Walker, Harley J. and William G. Haag. "Fred B. Kniffen on Matters Geographic," in *Geoscience and Man,* Vol. 5. Baton Rouge: Louisiana State University Press, 1974.

Whiffen, Marcus. *American Architecture Since 1780.* Cambridge: M.I.T. Press, 1969.

Wilson, Eugene M. *Alabama Folk Houses.* Montgomery: Alabama Historical Commission, 1975.

Zimiles, Martha and Murray. *Early American Mills.* New York: Bramhall House, 1973.

INDEX

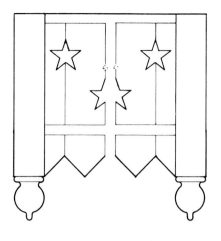

clg. ht.

The Architectural Legacy of the
Lower Chattahoochee Valley in Alabama and Georgia

was composed in VIP Garamond by

Bailey Typography, Inc., Nashville, Tennessee,

with display typeset in Caslon italic with swash

by Alexander Typesetting, Indianapolis, Indiana.

This book was printed by

Thomson-Shore, Inc., Dexter, Michigan,

and bound by John H. Dekker and Sons, Grand Rapids, Michigan.

At The University of Alabama Press,

the book was designed by Anna Fleck Jacobs,

and production was directed by Paul R. Kennedy.